The Arkansas Rockefeller

THE ARKANSAS ROCKEFELLER

John L. Ward

LOUISIANA STATE
UNIVERSITY PRESS
Baton Rouge and London

Copyright © 1978 by Louisiana State University Press
All rights reserved
Manufactured in the United States of America
Designer: Albert Crochet
Type face: VIP Primer
Typesetter: Graphic Composition, Inc., Athens, Georgia
Printer and Binder: Kingsport Press, Inc., Kingsport, Tennessee

Library of Congress Cataloging in Publication Data

Ward, John L   1930–
    The Arkansas Rockefeller.

    Bibliography: p.
    Includes index.
    1. Rockefeller, Winthrop, 1912–1973
2. Arkansas—Governors—Biography. 3. Arkansas—
Politics and government—1951–   I. Title.
F415.3.R62W37   976.7'05'0924   [B]   75–5354
ISBN 0–8071–0253–9

Contents

Illustrations

Preface

I served as director of public relations for Winthrop Rockefeller from May, 1964, until 1971, directing the governor's successful reelection campaign in 1968; and participated in a major policy way in the other campaigns. Material for this book has been gathered from several sources, including extensive interviews with Mr. Rockefeller a few months after his leaving office and before he learned he was seriously ill; interviews with Mrs. Jeannette Rockefeller, his wife during his years in public life, and interviews with some twenty-five other persons who worked for him, with him, or against him during the build-up of his campaign organization and while he served as governor. In addition to these sources, Mr. Rockefeller made available to me the materials contained in his Archives—correspondence, memoranda, newspaper clippings, tape-recorded speeches, and other such things relating to his public life. Opinion surveys by several pollsters, including Joe Belden of Dallas, Texas, and Eugene Newsom of Little Rock, Arkansas, have also been used extensively; these documents are likewise housed in the Archives.

Introduction

He couldn't be figured, not even from the very beginning. He looked and acted like a visitor from another world in Arkansas—inevitably and irrevocably in conflict because he was different philosophically, socially, economically, culturally, genetically. He had cultivated, Yankee manners and tastes, augmented by a continental courtliness, by the considerable refinements of his family, and by a splash of New York night life—all this transplanted into what must have seemed a barren social wasteland: Arkansas in 1953.

Winthrop Rockefeller was a Yale dropout who had worked in the Texas oil fields and spent six years in the infantry. He had also been all over the world in the company of kings, princes, prime ministers, sheiks, and social idols. Now he was living and working among people who mostly hadn't been more than three hundred miles from home in their lives.

He was a big hulk of a man, moving with indefatigable purpose, but awkwardly, along the unfamiliar and frequently unkind highways of Arkansas politics and public life. Campaigning, he looked as open as a book, allowing people to peer curiously into his face and squeeze his big hand as he stooped awkwardly and nervously over them; but they didn't know the real Rockefeller.

He was called "prissy sissy" and "Madison Avenue Cowboy" by his enemies, and he really didn't know how to handle these appellations that were part of the rhetoric of Arkansas politics. To him, politics was never a game, and that got him into lots of trouble because it robbed him of the resilience and flexibility that was a source of strength in those he fought against. Each double cross, each discourtesy, each stinging charge, each setback at the hands of some politician on a self-serving mission went right to his insides and stayed there, chewing him up like the proverbial fox under the good man's coat. More often than not, when he tried to retaliate with some name-calling of his own, it backfired, because he was inept at it. And he was never proud of what he had said out of hurt or anger. He believed a man's word was his bond, and he never quite became reconciled to the fact that he had pledged not to seek a third term, then broke that pledge and ran again.

To many Arkansans he always seemed the casual shopper looking over the state as he might examine a golden bangle at Tiffany's, likely to put it back down on the counter after a while and go somewhere else. He was a Republican in a state full of Democrats and a very rich man in a poor state. He was a night person, with a keen but unusual sense of humor. He was left-handed and maddeningly stubborn. He used an aftershave lotion that was definitely not available at the corner grocery, and this was equally true of the cigarettes he virtually chain-smoked. He ate and drank things regularly that most Arkansans had never even heard of; but, on the other hand, he could spread peanut butter on crackers or cookies and make a meal of it. He had an irritating tendency to forget some important things completely and an uncanny capacity for remembering the smallest details of others. He was almost never on time anywhere, yet in other ways he could show a genuine concern for people's rights and conveniences that was as out of place as it was correct and sincere.

All these things set him apart, but they didn't count for much when measured against the big difference, the thing that outweighed everything else altogether. His name was Rockefeller. To Arkansans, he was Rockefeller—grandfather, father, son, brothers, the Foundation, Standard Oil, everything. Yet, he did not fit the Rockefeller family mold either. In fact, not much about him fit. Philosophically, he was too liberal—particularly on the race issue—for most Arkansans. Physically, at 6′ 4″ and 240 pounds, he loomed over almost everyone. And the high heels on his custom-made cowboy boots didn't help. The most formal function did not cause him to forsake those boots, and his cowman's hat also became a trademark. He didn't hide the fact that he took a drink, lived atop the highest mountain in Central Arkansas, and went about his business in a private jet.

He answered questions with bold, often politically hazardous candor; and he had a penchant for circumventing stereotyped tradition and authority in his gleeful challenges to sacred cows and self-serving leaders. He could not have been a "typical" politician if he had tried—and he certainly did not try. Indeed, his reasons for wanting to become—and tenaciously overcoming every obstacle in order to become—governor of Arkansas remain a fascinating riddle to those who helped elect him. Why did he subject himself to the abuse of politics, southern-style? Why did he take on the vexations of a state burdened with inadequate resources—financial and otherwise—nineteenth-century legislative thinking, and little hope for improvement? His idea and the people's idea of why he was in Arkansas seemed poles apart. He could not tell them. He lacked that skill in communication, lacked that understanding of their daily language. Neither could they tell him of their hopes and dreams, of their selfishness nurtured in poverty and hardened against the blunt edge of political power and exploitation. They saw him as a stranger they would never know or understand because they had nothing with which to compare him. And he, with all his experience and contact with the peoples of the world—he saw them as strangers too. Yet, he needed them, in a way that he had never needed anyone before.

It frustrated him to realize that these people of Arkansas,

with their provincial attitudes and their rigidly conservative opinions, would define for him in a large sense his own boundaries. Winthrop Rockefeller had mostly ordered his own world throughout his adult life. Now, in seeking to govern, he would be governed—by these people whose willingness to accept him as a man and a leader would determine precisely how far he could go in achieving his goals.

His administration was characterized by progressive ideas, many of which could not be implemented during his two terms. It was also marked by controversy and clamor from Republicans and Democrats alike. But many of the programs he initiated and championed—and lost—were put through by his successor, whose proposals to the general assembly were called, with a good deal of accuracy, "the Rockefeller program with a smile."

Rockefeller's smile during his tenure became more grim as many of his programs went down in a general assembly that would chorus to the Republican governor at the close of his first legislative session, to the tune of "This Old House":

> These old halls may shake and tremble,
> this old world may turn out flat;
> But 'til Hell is frozen solid,
> I remain a Democrat.

They did, and so did Arkansas. But despite all the obstacles, Rockefeller got through more reform legislation than had been accomplished during any preceding four-year period in Arkansas history.

Yet to some of the legislators Rockefeller forever remained a plague, spreading down from the North, so to speak, to be endured but never succumbed to. One state senator said Winthrop Rockefeller was like a case of the measles: "We might as well have it and get it over with." How could he, as basically shy as he was, overcome all this? How could he push his way forward to the political table and then stubbornly pour every ounce of leadership and energy he possessed, and as much as it took of his wealth, into an effort to make his fellow-Arkansans accept him and what he represented?

Orval Faubus, his predecessor, said after Rockefeller left office: "At the time Rockefeller ran in 1964, Arkansas was the strongest Democratic state in the Union." Faubus praised WR's audacity and courage in seeking to break down political tradition. It was a new beginning for Rockefeller and for Arkansas. The people had arrived at their own decision—independently—and they were ready for a change, for that breath of fresh air they eventually saw in Rockefeller. Republicanism was pretty radical change, all right, but they were ready to go even that far to show their mettle. They didn't know where it would lead, of course, except that they were convinced that with Rockefeller they would go places they had never been before. He did not disappoint them.

Why was Rockefeller defeated? Why had he won in the first place? Did he really change things? Did he really create a two-party system in a state 85 percent Democratic? Did he successfully fight what he called "Arkansas' vast inferiority complex"? Or did Rockefeller, by raising hopes and by using large amounts of his personal fortune to improve state government as though it were a worthy charity, leave Arkansas a more troubled state than he found it? This book will attempt to answer these and other questions. One thing is certain: Arkansas will never be the same again.

The Arkansas Rockefeller

CHAPTER I

Selling the Two-Party System

Winthrop Rockefeller's coming to Arkansas in the first place wasn't especially dramatic, except perhaps in retrospect. Persons close to him who knew the story sometimes laughingly referred to the move here as one made "under cover of darkness." In reality, he simply packed up his red Cadillac, recruited his longtime associate and friend, Jimmy Hudson (who was black), and headed for Little Rock. He put up at the Sam Peck Hotel while he searched out the proper place to put down his permanent roots.

His early years had not been altogether promising, though he had proved to himself that he was equal to the task of making it the hard way in the Texas oil fields and in the infantry. During his military service he distinguished himself for the full span of his six-year stint. He joined as a private shortly before World War II began and rose to the rank of lieutenant colonel. He was with the Seventy-Seventh Division in the Pacific, and found himself the senior officer left alive after a suicide plane attack on the troop ship U.S.S. *Henrico*. Though injured, Rockefeller took command until he was relieved the next day, spent six weeks in a hospital, and then returned to active duty again, only to be stricken with infectious hepatitis.[1]

After the war he toured the United States at the request of the secretary of war, to survey and make recommendations on the adjustment problems of veterans. He made his report and left the service, having earned the Bronze Star with clusters and the Purple Heart, among other decorations. He is in the Infantry Officer Hall of Fame at Ft. Benning, Georgia.

In 1948, during his "playboy" days in New York, Rocke-feller married Barbara "Bobo" Sears. In 1964, he would readily acknowledge that if a person wished to look him up in newspaper files, he quite possibly would be listed under the heading "Playboy," but he said his life was hardly so simple as that. Before he left New York, he was involved in many other activities, but they didn't receive much attention then because of other publicity. The Rockefellers were the subjects of a stormy divorce in 1954 that garnered Winthrop many pages in the lurid magazines of the day, as well as in other publications.

In 1953 an army buddy, the late Frank Newell of Little Rock, had convinced Rockefeller that he should come to Arkansas. Rockefeller did come and found there just what he wanted; he bought 927 acres atop Petit Jean Mountain. It was overgrown, thin soil, but Rockefeller set to work on it with abandon. Yet, even then, Rockefeller was not content just to farm, however challenging that might be. His interests covered a wide span; he got involved in home-building and a number of other endeavors under the um-brella of a company he formed called Winrock Enter-prises.[2] His philanthropies also commanded much of his time and resources. He financed the building of a model school at Morrilton, which represented an investment of his own resources totaling $1.2 million; and he and his second wife—the former Jeannette Edris, whom he had married in 1956—led in efforts to build a new arts center in Little Rock, a $1-million effort. For three years he under-wrote the operating costs for a medical clinic in Perry County, perhaps one of the poorest of Arkansas' seventy-five counties; and he made many gifts annually to the state's institutions of higher education, as well as to some institutions elsewhere in the United States. He provided many scholarships for deserving high school students, and that program continues under the aegis of the Winthrop Rockefeller Foundation.

Winrock remained the focal point of his interests, however. It was where he began in Arkansas, and where he
always wanted to return. During a celebration of his first
ten years in Arkansas, attended by several members of his
family and hundreds of Arkansans, he told this little story
about the farm:

> My brother Laurance came down here when we were really
> just biting into the land at Petit Jean Mountain. As a matter of
> fact, those eight bulldozers put up a plume of dust in the
> drought period which you could see from 20 to 50 miles. Laur-
> ance, who is the brother between Nelson and myself, has a
> tremendous sense of humor, a little saccharine sometimes; but
> after we came back and he had appropriately washed the dust
> out of his throat, he sat there holding his glass in his hand and
> he said to me, "Winnie, you know all my young life I have been
> told that the country life is the simple life, but after what I've
> seen today, it's a lot of goddamn foolishness."[3]

There would be more foolishness, with more substance
than friendly banter between brothers, as Rockefeller's
public service to Arkansas increased. There was to be hos-
tility and frustration, much of it emanating from the floors
of Arkansas' house and senate.

Representative John Miller, a small man from the hill
country of Melbourne, broke into tears on the house floor
more than once during Rockefeller's tenure. Nudes—created by art students at state-supported institutions and
displayed in the capitol along with other paintings—drew
Miller's condemnation, and his tears on one occasion. The
drawings seemed to reflect, for Miller and those like him,
the permissiveness that came in with Rockefeller. Miller,
loudly indignant, went before the legislative council to
plead his case; he described the exhibit as nothing more
than nudes depicted in vulgar and distasteful poses.[4] The
council debated the matter briefly, and one cautious
member, aware that the exhibit was part of the Arkansas
Festival of Arts, wondered if they ought to study the paint-

ings before deciding what to do. "You know whether you are for nekkid women being painted with everything showing and hung in the State Capitol!" Miller shouted at him. The legislators were persuaded, and officially expressed disapproval.

Earlier, in March of 1967, with the new Republican governor only three months into his first term, Miller's sensibilities had been wounded. A provoked and frustrated governor had commented, at the end of a harried day trying to get some of his program through the legislature, "I wish that bunch of bastards would go home." Miller was on the house floor the next day, and he was unable to repeat the word uttered by the governor. "It starts with a 'b' and ends with an 's' and is plural," he explained carefully but with considerable emotion. "It really disturbs me when the chief executive of our state calls me something that reflects on my mother." Miller was crying by now. "I think that man should apologize to this House . . . and at the same time tell my mother and your mother that he is sorry he reflected on their character." Miller received a standing ovation.[5]

Thus was the conflict between the governor and the legislature symbolized, and thus did Miller represent the kind of thinking that was so different from the governor's but with which the governor must deal. There was trouble brewing between Rockefeller and the legislators that would have repercussions almost everywhere. It was an abrasive time in Arkansas. But things had begun to change the moment this man arrived.

He had hardly unpacked the Cadillac when he was invited into things. One invitation Rockefeller accepted from the Faubus administration in 1955 changed the face of Arkansas for all time, availing Rockefeller of the opportunity to lead Arkansas into a period of industrial and economic growth that would be the envy of the South. As chairman of the newly formed Arkansas Industrial Development

Commission (AIDC), WR immediately brought professionals and professionalism into the picture. Results came quickly. Here was a man who could confront anyone anywhere on an equal basis. His fellow Arkansans got the picture at once, and they responded through the legislature in 1957 with a resolution declaring "the confidence and appreciation of all the people in the high accomplishments, able leadership and personal generosity of Winthrop Rockefeller."[6] As governor, Faubus signed the resolution, but the time came when he must have wondered whether that had been so wise after all.

Nevertheless, except during the fiercest political struggles, Rockefeller and Faubus seemed to enjoy each other. Their exchanges were often marked by humor, as in these letters in 1960.[7] On March 9 of that year, Faubus wrote Rockefeller that he was reappointing him to the Arkansas Industrial Development Commission and asked that Rockefeller remit one dollar to the secretary of state's office in order to obtain the commission and duplicate oath. Rockefeller answered: "I am happy to advise you that I was able to raise one dollar to send forthwith to the Secretary of State." Faubus replied to this with, "I was afraid I would have to loan you a dollar so that you could pay the fee with the Secretary of State and thus qualify for reappointment and thus continue service on the AIDC board. Therefore, I am glad to learn that you were able to raise the dollar to make the payment. I will now dismiss this serious problem from my mind, and look forward to continued service to the people of Arkansas, along with you, as one of my able associates."

There was considerable interest in Rockefeller's politics and the role he might take. In the election year of 1960, as the day neared, Rockefeller explained that he had had a frank discussion with Governor Faubus and had "told him that I expect to support the Republican Party in the forthcoming campaign and his opponent, Mr. Henry Britt, in the gubernatorial race. Because of my role in the AIDC, I felt it proper to give the governor such notice and I have every reason to believe he understands my position."[8] Actually, Faubus wasn't really concerned about the miniscule GOP as a serious challenge. And Britt, a Hot Springs lawyer, didn't worry the incumbent governor at all. But Rockefeller worried him; and his worries were shared by others. When Britt was thoroughly defeated at the polls, as had been expected, Rockefeller went beyond the usual post-election pledge to do better next time.

In many speeches, what he said was properly taken as a warning among those he would later oppose. Rockefeller knew that the job of building a strong, constructive second party would be a longterm project. He had warned as much in a speech on radio and television a month before the election, saying:

> When I advocate an active, virile two-party system I do so in the firm conviction that Arkansas as a state and Arkansans as individuals will benefit from it. Your freedom will be expanded. Your horizons will be broadened. And we will achieve a new significance in the Nation. We will cease being taken for granted. I urge you to join in the work that lies ahead—not just two or four years ahead, but in the immediate future, to construct a meaningful, exciting second party for this great state. There are marvelous times ahead for free Americans, for free Arkansans. Be part of them.[9]

It wasn't long before this Republican in name—Rockefeller—began to make noises like a Republican in fact, and the "boys" in the legislature, not to speak of many other officeholders, began to get nervous. "The time is coming," warned Perry County Representative Paul Van Dalsem, "when you will have to choose between Winthrop Rockefeller and Orval Faubus. He put money in the counties and gave you boys opposition. Just who in hell does Mr. Rockefeller think he is that he can play both sides?"[10]

This was a pretty strong statement, even for 1963 and

even after Rockefeller's interest in politics began to irritate some. People in power were getting more nervous by the minute, and they soon launched a move to sink Rockefeller. He was pumping life into the Republican party, and they could see opposition developing at the ballot box for every legislator, every county official, and the governor himself. It was too much. "We just can't see a Republican Party leader as chairman of that commission. We think the commission should be dominated by Democrats in the state," Walter Day, an eastern Arkansas representative, said.[11] Some of the legislators wanted to withhold the AIDC appropriation until Rockefeller left. Others suggested dissolving the existing commission and appointing a new one, *sans* Rockefeller. Either way, Rockefeller would be ousted, and good riddance, they thought.

Faubus got into the act with a bit of his characteristic caution. "Rockefeller's political position has its drawbacks," he acknowledged carefully in an interview. "For example, some members of the all-Democratic congressional delegation don't like the idea of a Republican getting credit for Democratic-sponsored programs." Faubus roped in a favorite political pony when he wanted to trample around a bit on Rockefeller—his brother Nelson. On this occasion he mentioned that Nelson Rockefeller was grooming himself to run against John F. Kennedy for president and suggested, "It's my thinking that Winthrop Rockefeller will spend the next two years looking after the interests of his brother. I wonder how much he will be concerned about being the head of the AIDC?"[12]

WR was a trifle annoyed. Faubus' comments, he said, were "illogical and out of perspective."[13] A friend of both men told Rockefeller privately, however—after an impromptu poll in the house—not to worry because there wasn't much trouble in the house membership as a whole. At that point, Rockefeller was still too naive politically to realize that lots of lawmakers would destroy a good program at the drop of a hat in exchange for political power and advantage. Public sentiment began to surface. Comments by Van Dalsem and other old-guard detractors in the house became more shrill. The Arkansas chapter of the American Association of University Women adopted a resolution supporting Rockefeller, and the president of the Little Rock Industrial Development Company made a strong statement in his behalf. Somebody introduced a resolution in the house praising Rockefeller, but it was quickly voted down. Former governor McMath called the attempt "the height of ingratitude," and a statewide newspaper reported that a counter movement to "save Rockefeller" was having some effect on Faubus.[14]

Rockefeller described himself as "an innocent bystander" in the hassle. As public sentiment swelled in his favor, he began talking more specifically of the Republican party's future in Arkansas. "I don't intend to let the opportunity drop," said Rockefeller, hinting broadly. "We're entitled to better government in Arkansas."[15] The flood of letters and telegrams and phone calls supporting WR continued. At the University of Arkansas, Faubus was hanged in effigy, and in Little Rock the governor from the hills of northwest Arkansas tried to call a halt to the efforts against Rockefeller.

On March 28, 1964, Rockefeller—having won the fight—tendered his resignation from the AIDC chairmanship, but the move didn't plunk any chords of happiness among his detractors. They knew what was coming. WR was going to run for governor. Many legislators were relieved about one thing, though. They didn't have to go on record for or against Rockefeller.

Jeannette Rockefeller, his fiery-tempered but intensely dedicated wife during those years of his rise to political power and the holding of it, recalls that Rockefeller didn't want it.

He knew this was going to create havoc with his private life. He knew it was going to be psychologically difficult to get out and be a public person when he'd been a private person. Up to that time, he had after all run his own business his own way and he had been able to say yes or no or do exactly as he pleased. He was going to have to beg instead of tell. At the same time, overriding everything else was what he felt Arkansas needed. As long as he was the only person who could put over the philosophy, there he was—stuck. He came to me and asked me what I felt. I said I knew it was going to be difficult, but that this was a decision that he would have to make for himself . . . and that whatever he decided, I would go along with it and do my best to help.[16]

When Rockefeller began his move to revitalize the Republican party, as both he and Mrs. Rockefeller had predicted, he was not welcomed with open arms by all the party faithful. There were lots of party functionaries who had worked out a comfortable way to "live with" the Democrats in their home counties; and functionaries and hierarchy alike enjoyed carving up the patronage pie whenever a Republican administration took up residence in Washington.

So it was that Bill Spicer of Fort Smith, state chairman of the Republican party, had mixed emotions as he made a great show of cooperation and brotherly love when Rockefeller decided to cut himself into a bit of the action in the waning days of the Eisenhower administration. Spicer's ebullience would soon turn to venom as Rockefeller continued to punch his way into the GOP control room. Marion Burton—on loan from Rockefeller to serve as executive assistant to Spicer—expressed himself on the matter with a strong letter to Spicer: "Up to the time that you took the position of working against the national committeeman [Rockefeller how held that post] and the assistant to the national committeeman [Everett Ham] you received nothing but help, cooperation and encouragement from personnel in the state headquarters and especially from the national committeeman and Everett Ham." [17]

Burton, a young lawyer, charged Spicer with various areas of party neglect and noted that the Republican party was growing in Arkansas, notwithstanding what Burton called "narrow interests." The truth was, Spicer hated Ham, whom he considered tasteless, arrogant, overbearing, and not too intelligent about politics. Ham, employed by the department of agriculture before he joined forces with Rockefeller, was a large man with a crew cut, whose total dedication was to Rockefeller and the Republican party. He could be—and frequently was—quite heavy-handed, excusing it in the name of building a two-party system. Ham knew how to roll heads, and he did it. You could go with Rockefeller or get out of the way. The old mossback Republicans did neither. They just got stomped down by the growing numbers of Rockefeller supporters.

Spicer's way of dealing with the Rockefeller-Ham-Burton juggernaut was to try to build stronger ties with Republicans over the state. A friend of Spicer's in northwest Arkansas, Walter Stouffer, Jr., wrote a lengthy letter directed to "Fellow Republicans" that included these comments: [18]

> I have had a lengthy conference . . . at their [Ham's and Burton's] request. We discussed the present rift at great length. . . . I feel it is my duty as a Republican to report to you. . . . Mr. Ham showed me a map of Arkansas with each county that he felt was favorable to his faction in red. He informed me that when he had all or the majority of the counties in his column, he could act in regard to his plans for the Republican Party in the future. . . . I feel his plans include replacing all county and state officials at his discretion. . . . He also told me he wanted Mr. Rockefeller to run for governor. I asked Mr. Ham to remain inactive for a short period of time so that this rift could be eliminated. He informed me that he would not, but would start a vigorous program to work against Bill Spicer and the state organization. . . . Let these moves for power be

aimed at our position in state politics, rather than toward satisfaction of any select person or persons.

The letter seemed to summarize the feelings of resentment and bitterness on the part of some of the GOP old guard toward Rockefeller and his increasing entourage of aides and supporters. Spicer wrote a letter to a friend of Rockefeller's on October 15, 1963, describing the frustration between the old Republicans and the new. The letter to George Hinman, New York Republican national committeeman, stated in part:[19] "It is interesting to note the activities of some of the boys operating in Arkansas. I have never seen so many moves being made by the wrong people, in the wrong manner, at the wrong time." Spicer included a copy of Stouffer's letter and said his friend had the "pulsebeat" of the people of Arkansas. "We have a hard core of trueblue Republicans who will stand pat . . . regardless of the pressures and tempting offers presented," Spicer wrote. Rockefeller was given a copy of this letter.

A few weeks later, Spicer wrote Ab Herman (who was director of political organization for the national party), revealing his frustration that the national party seemed to be maintaining contacts and making arrangements in Arkansas without his knowledge. Spicer asked Herman to verify that he was being circumvented in favor of Rockefeller. "It is most unfortunate," Spicer said, "to experience this disunity and turmoil in the Republican Party in Arkansas. Every effort has been made to work as a team. Since this is not desired by some of the people, there is one remaining thing for the state organization to do, proceed as we wish and let the opposition spin their wheels. Time usually corrects errors and mistakes. Without question this will transpire in Arkansas, too."[20]

Spicer sent Rockefeller a copy of the letter, to which Rockefeller felt obliged to respond on December 18, 1963, with this comment: "I am sorry that you felt impelled to seek this information by a letter to the national office when the answer could have been so easily obtained by either a phone call or a letter to me."[21]

Spicer didn't appreciate Rockefeller's remarks, and a few weeks later he wrote a letter to a couple of leading Republicans—John Paul Hammerschmidt of Harrison and Gene Holman of DeQueen—acknowledging their desire to "see the troubles in the party solved" and reporting that he had met at length with Rockefeller, but that no progress had been made. Spicer stated in his letter that he knew there were efforts underway to get rid of him. But, he said, he wasn't worried; when he stepped aside it would be his own decision and not the action of the opposition. Spicer expressed disbelief that any Republican would seek the office of governor without the full support of the state organization. "Least of all," the GOP chairman went on, "would I think Winthrop would seek such a position under the current political climate. It is true he may have thoughts of attaining such an office and avoiding the support of the party. Should this be the situation, he will have to learn the hard way."[22]

Spicer wanted Ham out of the way, if not fired, and he suggested that Burton would be a good man to elevate to the post of assistant to the national committeeman in Ham's place. However, Spicer observed that Burton had gotten "out on Cloud 9 a few times." The state chairman ended his letter with the observation that the "regular Republicans" had operated the Arkansas Republican party in past years, "they are doing so now. They will be doing so next week—month—year." But Spicer soon changed his tune. Shortly after he wrote his letter to Hammerschmidt and Holman, he and Rockefeller talked by phone. The tension between them was evident. In a memo written for Rockefeller's files, Spicer's comments reflected defeat.[23] Rockefeller's remarks exuded the feeling of victory and a rather weak interest in forging a cooperative relationship once the smoke cleared, but that effort failed.

Rockefeller noted that when he wanted to know about

some details, Spicer had responded curtly: "The party rules have been circumvented so many times [meaning by Ham and Rockefeller] I don't know that it's important." In regard to the upcoming Republican meeting, Spicer said, "I seriously doubt that any other than those known as the people on the 'Rockefeller' side of the argument would be there. You would have the majority. That's been demonstrated before. In fact, I don't know that I would bother to go." Rockefeller said he didn't see "any point in a battle between the factions within the party. My hope would be that you would take the attitude that 'here we are; let's get on with the business.'" The national committeeman went on to suggest that "if I were in your shoes I would be inclined to say, in order to get on with the business and avoid further fights, 'Come and discuss our plans with the idea that if our plans are not acceptable we will listen to other points of view.'" Spicer said he was approaching the point within the organization of saying "to hell with it." He charged Rockefeller with taking control of the party.

And so he had.

Rockefeller responded: "I know a majority who are sympathetic to my objectives—building on a grassroots basis," adding with a bit of a needle, "I think most of the people in that camp are not satisfied that is the objective of the faction that has rallied around you." Spicer shot back: "I believe in the grassroots also. Those points of irritation are still with us. They will be with us from now on. As far as Bill Spicer is concerned, I am rapidly reaching the point where I am going to wash my hands of the whole thing." Rockefeller sarcastically said that if he were Spicer he would substitute for that last phrase, "tender my resignation." After a few more exchanges, Spicer exploded: "It's the cotton-picking nutheads in your organization that are causing the trouble . . . your methods in the past—and I'm afraid they will continue—of letting people under you do the dirty work."

Rockefeller had already conceded in public comments

that one of the major obstacles to his political ambitions was the rift in the Republican party in Arkansas. Spicer had said publicly that Rockefeller's actions had "split the state party right down the middle," adding that "some of the boys are talking about putting our star quarterback on the bench." Ham said he had virtually gotten down on his knees and begged the Republicans on the other side of the rift to join the Rockefeller team, "but they weren't interested in new people."[24]

A longtime Arkansas GOP leader told a *Wall Street Journal* reporter, "Can you imagine the reaction of a 50- or 60-year-old Republican who's been spending his own time and money working at this to have some two-bit employee who's never succeeded at one thing [a reference to Ham] to come in and tell him what to do to win an election?"[25]

In an interview in 1972, Rockefeller looked back on Spicer this way:

> The basic problem was political philosophy coupled with enormous ego. His following was politically antagonistic to my basic philosophy. They were the right-wingers up to and including sometimes Birchers, and they were power-crazy. It went so far that when I finally forced Spicer to come to see me one time in Washington, he just announced to me that he didn't really know why he was bothering to sit down and talk with me about party plans in Arkansas because I had no influence, and as far as he was concerned, with the approaching state convention, I would be summarily relieved of my duties as Republican National Committeeman or I would no longer be the Republican National Committeeman. And I was a little shocked but retorted that I didn't quite understand what he was talking about because I had no intention of withdrawing from the office. And in his arrogance, he just announced that he controlled enough delegate votes to the state convention to replace me. When I came back from Washington, we looked into it. He probably at that minute was correct.[26]

Rockefeller put everything else aside and went to work on shifting that balance the other way. He succeeded, largely because groundwork had begun several years earlier. This takeover—and that's what it was—was the culmination of that evolution into a position of party responsibility and elective office. Because Rockefeller felt that the industrial and economic development of the state was being stymied by one-party politics, he organized the Committee for a Two-Party System and toured the state, talking about the two-party system.

The response was good; but Nelson Rockefeller cautioned his brother not to let the seeming success go to his head, explaining that half of the people had never seen a millionaire and the other half had perhaps heard the name Rockefeller but had never shaken hands with one. But the younger brother said repeatedly that he didn't care what brought these people to meetings as long as they came and listened.

They had begun to listen in earnest in October, 1960, when a "Party for Two Parties" filled three big barns and a tent at Winrock, launching the GOP effort in Arkansas. Entertainment included such notables as Edgar Bergen and Charlie McCarthy, Tex Ritter and Kathryn Grayson. The idea was to mix Democrats and Republicans together, let them see that neither group had horns, and raise some money for the upcoming Republican efforts at the same time. Admission was fifty dollars a person. At that, many hundreds showed up and the party was a success in more ways than one.

After the party, Rockefeller wrote members of his family to thank them for their contributions: "The concept of running for a two-party system—as against talking straight Republicanism—has been most effective, for in many parts of Arkansas the word 'Republican' is still a dirty word. Under the guise of a new name we have been able to bring out Independents and many Democrats who are disgruntled with the present situation."[27]

Rockefeller's reasons for involving himself in Arkansas

politics remain difficult to fathom, even now. He tried to explain it to himself and others many times; position papers stated his motives; political observers have speculated on the question; his family has commented, as have his many former aides; but so far, no one has shed any real light on why he did what he did.

If one could peel back the layers of complexity from his personality, the thing or things that compelled him to trudge up and down the dusty political roads might just be found among his earliest recollections of his mother and father and of the competitive spirit that was nurtured in him. His memories of those early years remained vivid throughout his life. And the lessons he learned from his parents in that period stayed with him best, perhaps because his relationship with his family became strained as he returned from the war and assumed a way of life that did not always conform to their ideas of how he ought to conduct himself. At any rate, I think it is safe to say that his reasons for seeking the governorship of his adopted state had little to do with whatever he might have learned *after* he got to Arkansas. Early in the 1960s he had begun to chafe at the way things were in Arkansas, politically and economically. And the "Party for Two Parties" was only the first shot in what would be a regular salvo, day by day and week by week, against the status quo.

As Mrs. Rockefeller recalled, "He would be able to go just so far, and then he'd come up against the blank wall of politics; so he sat down with himself and realized that if in truth that kind of progress that he envisioned for the state was going to happen . . . then something would have to be done . . . to break what had gone on all those years in terms of politics in Arkansas. At that point, the Republican Party was truthfully about five old men who sat on a porch until there was a Republican President and then held out their hands for some patronage. He wanted to work within the system and change things, activate the Republican Party, which he did at untold personal hurts."[28]

Harry Ashmore was one of those who saw Rockefeller from time to time in those days, and Ashmore—then editor of the *Arkansas Gazette* and later president of the Center for the Study of Democratic Institutions—remembers several conversations when WR "was gradually succumbing to the urge to get into politics with all four feet."[29] As Ashmore remembers it, he suggested to Rockefeller that he probably would be wise to avoid elective politics altogether, since the generally benign public attitude toward him as a disinterested benefactor was bound to dissipate in a partisan contest. But it was clear Rockefeller was beset by an ambition that couldn't be satisfied by attempting to shape public affairs through his private influence and personal financial resources. Ashmore was convinced that there was a large measure of altruism in Rockefeller's determination and that Rockefeller "genuinely wanted to be of service to the state he had adopted, and thought that he could bring to the governorship a valuable personal independence guaranteed by his protected position as a man of great wealth. His brother Nelson was doubtless his model, and perhaps a symbolic goad."[30]

Once Ashmore realized that Rockefeller was going to make the try, he urged him to run as a Democrat, since doing otherwise would surely increase the odds against him. "I pointed out," Ashmore said, "that he would have no ideological difficulty in finding a place in the Democratic spectrum, since the party was traditionally split into factions that ranged all the way from Left to Right." The usual lines had been blurred by Orval Faubus' injection of the emotional race issue; but as the tensions died down, Rockefeller might emerge as an essentially moderate healer, Ashmore believed. He had the advantages of an established position on race that would rally the black vote and attract much of Faubus' white opposition, a reputation as a sort of chamber of commerce progressive through his work with AIDC that would serve him well in the small towns, and a natural family attraction for the conservative

wealthy interests in the state. Ashmore remembers that
Rockefeller was "adamantly" against running as a Democrat. He said he supposed the reason was largely respect
for family tradition, plus the practical consideration that
his brother was a national Republican leader and a conten-
der for the GOP presidential nomination. WR's own idea
was that he might enter the race as an Independent.
Ashmore argued that this made no practical sense—that it
wouldn't really enhance Rockefeller's chances of election
and that it would deny him, if elected, any kind of national
political base. "Moreover," Ashmore added, "if he was
bound to invest his time, energy and money outside the
one-party system, I urged that he use it to try to build a
continuing, formal partisan opposition to the old Democratic statehouse machine, now nominally steered by Faubus, but largely harnessed to the services of Witt Ste-
phens [then president of Arkansas Louisiana Gas Co. and a
mostly behind-the-scenes political power] and his cohorts."[31]

Ashmore pointed out to Rockefeller that the label
"Democrat" no longer had its old magic, that Eisenhower
had received a heavy vote in the state, and that Faubus, for
all practical purposes, had bolted from the national Democratic party. "I told Winthrop," Ashmore recalled, "that I
doubted that he could be elected as a Republican, but that
if he took over the moribund party apparatus and headed a
state ticket that attracted able young men to stand for the
legislature and local office he might start a process that
would ultimately give state and local governments the
shaking up they badly needed."[32]

Rockefeller had gotten some contrary advice in October
of 1960, in an unsigned memorandum that was marked
with harsh and, it was hoped, discouraging words. The
writer acknowledged that no one had asked for his views or
his aid, and then went on to offer some of both.[33] He
had shared others' views, he said, about the lack of
and need for a second sound and effective political party

in Arkansas. But, he warned, "The course you are about to pursue in this direction is based upon many faulty bench-marks. The only end it can attain is complete frustration." According to the memo's author, Rockefeller's idea seemed to be to create a second effective political party by having Arkansas voters "rush out and support, vote for and contribute to Nixon and Britt." He went on to warn Rockefeller, "Precisely the measure of success you achieve in this direction, will be the hurt done to any hope for a constructive two-party system in the future." Rockefeller's critic decried the idea of massively reinforcing the central part of party structure.

It long since proved itself a complete barrier to any serious effort to create a second effective political party. The structure of the Republican Party methodology in Arkansas is a Kremlin-type apparatus on a scale most minuscular. Leaders of the Republican Party have clung to the party practices of the early post-bellum days with as great tenacity as the Democrats have to their mortal dread of integration. Now a federal (therefore a Republican) court has ordered enlightenment to remove the latter grim spectre on the ground of civil rights. No higher authority exists to direct abolition of the former, on grounds of moral rights and obligations. What again, in effect, you and the Republican Party are saying is, "You the electorate must support this candidate while at the moment you are denying completely and forever the privilege of the voters to participate in the selection of the candidate they must support. Democrats don't think that way." You are saying, "Let's all work for a two-party system; here's how we'll do it. We are Republicans and can offer you Democrats two alternatives. You can cast a protest vote, or a vote for the nominee of the second party." You are telling me the way to create a two-party system is to persuade people to vote for a second party, because it is a second party. In the name of a two-party system you ask me to vote for a candidate for President— Nixon—whom I completely distrust. You ask me to vote for a candidate for governor and do not give me one reason why I should do it, except that he is a Republican. I don't vote that way, whether he be Democrat or Republican.[34]

But distrust had marked the entry of Rockefeller into

party affairs, mostly because of Everett Ham—the hard-nosed realist who could plot strategy this way: "I deliberately made fights in the counties on the theory that if you get a group fighting, they are fighting within the party and they are bringing more people in all the time and you are growing."[35]

Did Rockefeller know Ham was stirring up trouble this way? "No, not per se," Ham answered. "I don't think he would have gone along with that concept as such because Win didn't like to get people inflamed. He would take the more commonsense approach of reason. But I needed people excited so they would do something."

Tom Eisele, longtime friend and adviser to Rockefeller and a Republican leader (now a federal judge in Little Rock) remembers Ham's role in the early stages of party building this way: "As ruthless as he was, there was no possibility of Win Rockefeller having an imprint on the Republican Party until the machinery of the party was taken out of the hands of the Democrats and the Faubus people and the people who really had no interest in building a two-party system."[36]

Rockefeller explained later that "even though I had become Republican National Committeeman and had campaigned for Bubs Ricketts [GOP candidate for governor in 1962] and some of the others, my major thrust in the political field really was toward selling the two-party system." WR said he would like to be remembered in politics for his involvement in two-party activity. "I became involved as a candidate because of the two-party thrust."[37]

WR and Bobo Sears Rockefeller, shortly after their wedding in 1948.

WR campaigning in 1964.

WR rolls up his sleeves after a country store visit during the 1964 campaign.

On a visit during the 1964 campaign to Cherokee Village, a retirement community in northern Arkansas, WR posed for an amateur photographer.

WR speaking in front of his campaign bus in 1964.

Tom Eisele, campaign director, and Everett Ham, WR's aide, discuss the campaign with WR.

WR ties a youngster's shoelace
during the 1966 campaign.

WR in his role as cattleman, at his Winrock farm office, 1966.

Election night, 1966, WR and Maurice "Footsie" Britt pose for
photographers with an air of confidence.

WR calls on Orval Faubus shortly after being elected governor.

Inauguration day, 1967, in the governor's office. From left, stepdaughter Anne Bartley, John D. Rockefeller III, Winthrop Paul Rockefeller, Mrs. Bruce Bartley, and WR's wife Jeannette.

WR speaking at the memorial service for Martin Luther King, Jr., on the steps of the capitol.

Courtesy *Arkansas Democrat*

WR and Marion Crank debating on television, 1968.

At the opening of the state GOP headquarters in 1968, Marion Hotel.

CHAPTER II

The First Election

Rockefeller "tried every way in the world" to get others to run for governor in 1964, until finally everyone turned to him and asked, "What about you?" Rockefeller said he would, but he warned in tones that time has given the ring of prophesy, "Of course, we'll have to do it twice because we're not going to win the first time."[1]

Meanwhile, Faubus figured he'd get a lot of Republican votes because he always had. But he knew that Rockefeller represented the best hope for the Republicans to win the state's highest office. And it did look as if the Democratic party must go to work in earnest. The Republicans were enthusiastic. For the first time ever, they really believed that with Rockefeller they had a chance to win.

Rockefeller established his own ground rules early in the political game. I was hired, despite my inexperience, as WR's public relations director, and Joe Belden of Dallas was his pollster. In 1964 we were engaged on a conference call to discuss a poll. Rockefeller was speaking from his living room at Winrock, Belden was in Dallas, and I was in Little Rock. A number of questions that seemed appropriate for the survey had been rehearsed, but I remembered one other thing. When Rockefeller and Belden had suggested all the questions they thought should be asked in the poll, I added: "Let's ask the people what they think about WR's boots and hat."

There was a pause. Rockefeller said, "Go ahead and ask if you like but I don't give a goddamn what they think. Those boots and hat are a part of me and the people can accept me or turn me down but I will not change the way I dress." I had no more questions to suggest, and that one wasn't included in the final draft of poll questions.

After Rockefeller got his campaign going, it began to be clear to knowledgeable Democrats that the luxury of sitting back and watching would not be possible this time. There were complaints that even the gridiron exploits of the Arkansas razorbacks would have to take lower priority while Democratic attention turned to this upstart bunch of Republicans led by Rockefeller. Until then the word *uppity* had generally been reserved for Negroes who seemed bent on being somewhere other than in "their place." Now it was applied to Republicans as well. At any rate, Rockefeller was going to demonstrate his ability to get it all together and eventually win the governorship, though his prophecy about the first effort would hold.

Arguments about who was responsible for Rockefeller's victories—Democrats or Republicans—were never settled to the satisfaction of those down there in the lists, fighting it out. Even the evangelism of Rockefeller himself failed to convert to Republicanism many of those closely surrounding him. That is in part why organizations like Democrats for Rockefeller (DFR) were formed—to provide a home for the masses of people who could be for Rockefeller but were not Republicans, and not about to become Republicans. Needless to say, the DFR was much resented by many Republicans whose worst fears were realized when Rockefeller began appointing Democrats to positions in state government the minute he became governor. This, Ham was wont to point out, gave folks "no reason to want to become Republicans."

Sid McMath, the former governor, said several years afterward: "He had people in every community willing to go out and work for him. They were Rockefeller people, personally loyal. These people didn't care too much about party labels. They thought he was best for Arkansas."[2] But

Rockefeller, for all the seeming contradictions in his efforts and decisions, was genuinely interested in developing a strong grass-roots party. He just didn't get any help from those around him. It was a short-lived pride that enabled him to note, after his victory in 1966, "More Republican candidates ran in 1966 than had run collectively since the War Between the States." Republicans still weren't palatable to the people. That fact gave intense energy to a major internal fight that began shaping up as the 1964 campaign organization was being formed. The issue overtly would be Barry Goldwater, although the roots of the differences of opinion and philosophy went deeper and wider than that. Eisele, the campaign director, and Ham, WR's aide, were the principals—with Eisele not too keen on Goldwater and Ham at the opposite pole.

Tom Eisele was generally an easy man to get along with, most accommodating, although throughout the 1964 campaign he carried a stack of unanswered telephone-call slips in his pocket that would have choked a horse. Ham had thought, and hoped, that Eisele—a busy young attorney—would have little time to bother himself with the campaign; and Ham encouraged him into the effort, assuming that he, as assistant to the national committeeman, would actually call the shots and run the show. But Eisele didn't want to operate that way. He shut down his law practice and joined the campaign full time. Ham was dismayed.

The fact that Eisele wasn't a terribly good organizer and couldn't bring himself to bother very much with routine—even routine phone calls—didn't reduce the value of his enthusiasm and energy. In reality, his intelligence and the inspiration of his very presence in the organization were vital in the campaign effort. Next to WR's influence, Eisele was largely responsible for the degree of success that was achieved. On the other hand, Ham was generally a negative thinker, in my opinion, although he disagrees strongly with that description. He saw a major aspect of politics in terms of investigations and scandal and gumshoe operations, a game between private investigators and men with secret intelligence techniques. You must "know the enemy," he would argue. He did not inspire, but in his own way he was as dedicated to the effort as Eisele or anyone else. Ham had fulfilled his role early in the Rockefeller effort, having been instrumental in helping Rockefeller remove the old-guard Republicans who wouldn't cooperate. He thought he knew something about politics.

So Ham and Eisele were destined, perhaps, for the personality conflict that developed. The exchanges on the Goldwater matter were only the beginning. It became so intense, the argument about whether WR and Goldwater were to be "married" in political effort among Republicans, that Eisele threatened to resign—and would have if Rockefeller had sided with Ham. Rockefeller couldn't afford to lose Eisele, even though he may have felt privately that Ham's point of view was the more logical, or at least more consistent with his own past efforts with the party; but Rockefeller sided with Eisele.

The campaign director became progressively more irritated and frustrated by the efforts among old-guard Republicans to inject Goldwater into the Arkansas effort. Eisele felt, as did many in the campaign organization, that the presence of Goldwater in the campaign would drive away the more liberal-minded Independents and Democrats who were already supporting Rockefeller.

Ham, at that time Rockefeller's number one aide, was determined that Goldwater people would be in the Rockefeller campaign and that Goldwater's interests would be served by the Rockefeller campaign. Eisele—in a memorandum to Rockefeller that was remarkable for what it didn't say of his frustration and anger and his decision to resign if Rockefeller did not adhere to what he believed was the right course—wrote on August 5, 1964:

Decision on the relationship between the WR campaign and the Goldwater campaign must be made immediately if the MORE [Mobilization of Rockefeller Effort] program is to be successful. To date, all persons interested in the Rockefeller candidacy have been invited to work in the MORE program on the representation that they would be working solely for WR and that the Goldwater and WR campaigns would be kept separate [although coordinated in a friendly manner.] They are also being invited upon the theory that we are not working for local Republican candidates. If either of these policies is to be changed, such change should be made now before people are put to work who would not go forward under an arrangement where either Goldwater, or the local candidates, are "teamed up" with WR. Knowing that possible changes are in the air, it has made it difficult to proceed with the identification of MORE leadership. The last thing we need is a mass resignation of identified leaders upon announcement of a change in policy such as that indicated. It is better to wait until the change is decided upon and to obtain leaders who are sympathetic with a new policy, rather than to suffer the possible ill will from any leaders identified and accepted on the basis of the old policy.

Of course decisions on the policy questions referred to above have much broader significance than their application to the MORE program; but the MORE program is proceeding apace and every day additional people will be recruited for the organization. We run a definite risk of offending many of these people and demoralizing the organization by a failure to make a definite decision as to the character of the campaign at this time.[3]

Things didn't improve. Six days later Eisele wrote to WR:

I know that many of your strongest supporters are sincere in their belief that your identification with the national ticket will be very helpful. I share this view to a limited extent, but I believe that your support of Mr. Goldwater and your past statements are more than adequate to satisfy the true Republican Goldwater supporters. I am convinced that further efforts at identification will destroy our ability to obtain a large number of the Lyndon Johnson votes which will clearly be needed for victory. The fact is, that we must motivate these people to go to the polls and vote for you. It will not be enough for them to refrain from voting for Mr. Faubus. Everett [Ham] has given instructions . . . to alter the canvassing cards used in the MORE program to include the Goldwater . . . questions. Aside from the disruptional effect this will have upon the MORE workers, I feel that it will also introduce so much confusion as to make the canvass ineffectual and the results of little value to anyone. *Your* decision is needed immediately on this latter question. [Italics in original.]

On Eisele's memo of August 11, WR penciled this note: "For record, I agreed with GTE [Eisele] . . . my instructions were ignored."[4]

Ham acknowledged later that he had expected Eisele to be "more of a figurehead manager. I didn't envision him trying to run it. I thought that he would stay in his office and practice law and kind of let me run it. But he didn't see it that way. And I didn't make myself clear when I got him to be campaign manager."

Eisele recalled that he and others who stubbornly refused to allow intrusion of the Goldwater effort into the Rockefeller campaign "pretty well had the attitude [that we thought Goldwater shared] that generally they ought to be independent. I think some of the Goldwater advisors didn't think Rockefeller stood a chance. All the antagonisms developed late in the campaign, and there was some bitterness thereafter."

What did the public think of Rockefeller and what he was trying to do, from the first days of his political involvement in Arkansas? WR wanted to keep answers to that question, from the very beginning, and pollsters were working regularly in Arkansas on his behalf from the early 1960s through 1970. In October of 1960, it had already been observed that the possibility existed for a Republican to win a statewide election. One opinion survey for the Arkansas Democratic party asserted: "If the ballot carried the names of the two major candidates [Nixon and Kennedy] Nixon would probably push Kennedy fairly closely. If it were not for the States Righters, who managed to get on the ballot at the last minute, the Republicans would stand a fair to good chance of taking Arkansas for the first time in nearly a century."[5] This was in spite of the preponderance of traditional Democrats at the time the survey was made—66 percent of the electorate, in fact. Republicans represented only 12 percent, with the Independent category claiming 20 percent. Later, the Democratic and Independent figures would change markedly, as the pressure grew to elect Rockefeller, but there wouldn't be any significant swelling of Republican faithful.

It is significant that despite all of Rockefeller's claims and hopes that what was abuilding was not a personality cult but a Republican party, the percentage of persons calling themselves Republicans just didn't vary much from before WR got involved in party activities in the early 1960s to the day he left office in January of 1970. Pollster Belden found in February of 1961 that voters were quite aware of Rockefeller and that goodwill toward him was remarkably high; there was a leaning toward Rockefeller among blacks, Republicans, voters with business connections, and voters who didn't like Faubus.[6] There was a leaning away from Rockefeller among Democrats, voters with labor connections, and of course the voters who approved of Faubus. It was possible to read into all that some real potential for Rockefeller, although the same data led the pollster to comment: "Governor Faubus, of course, is bound to be a key force in the election. His hold on the electorate has weaknesses, but no one can deny that he continues to be the dominant figure in Arkansas, and his popularity is widespread. From the present evidence, he would be difficult to defeat should he decide to run for governor again." This came as no surprise to Rockefeller. "The development of two strong political parties in Arkansas finds a generally receptive climate," Belden continued, adding cautiously that whether this would strengthen the GOP "is something else."

But the nearer Rockefeller moved toward campaign time the weaker he seemed to become politically in the eyes of those he would look to for votes. In January of 1964, Belden advised Rockefeller that there had been a "hardening" of the Rockefeller image. WR's views were becoming better known as he was subjected to increasing political attacks. And the difficulty was intensified by the fact that most of the activity had been one-sided—against Rockefeller. Would the score change if Rockefeller took to the stump? He would see.

One thing had become evident—the incumbent governor would not simply walk back into the office. He was going to have to fight for his political life, and he had some awesome political liabilities to explain away. He had been in office five terms, too long in the eyes of many. Another big negative was that he had appointed every member of every one of the state's boards and commissions. And he had been the impetus behind a great deal of the legislation passed in recent sessions. Equally unsavory in the public eye was the fact that illegal gambling continued flagrantly, especially in Hot Springs and the Little Rock area.

Faubus, then, represented entrenched power, with all the abuses that attend it. And it would be against this entrenchment that Rockefeller would mount his attack. Virtually nobody thought Faubus would step down without another campaign, and most saw Rockefeller as the only person who could give the man from Greasy Creek a real rouser of a fight. It was going to be a fun time for the many thousands of Arkansans who loved politics and a good fight.

From 1961 to 1964, the 68 percent of Arkansans calling themselves Democrats had skidded to 48 percent, but the Republicans only gained from 11 to 13 percent. Independents rose from 17 percent to 35 percent. The margin was slim, but that 48 percent was under 50 for the first time, and Rockefeller and his organization took some comfort from that. Although none of the WR-financed polls ever showed it, there were reports from the Faubus camp that the two men were running neck and neck, at 48 percent each a couple of weeks before election day. At any rate, all polls showed that all other Republican candidates would lose miserably—and they did.[7]

It might have been possible for Rockefeller to win. Many believe so, and the fact that Faubus took to the stump like an evangelist convinced the second coming was two weeks hence certainly indicated that he felt such extreme measures were called for.

Much of Rockefeller's attack on Faubus was ineffective. High hopes had been pinned on the fact that Faubus had been in office too long, and WR pounded away on that all through the campaign. When it was over, only about 40 percent of the people felt the issue helped WR, and 24 percent of them thought it helped Faubus. Rockefeller hammered away about education, how vital it was that the state do a better job of equipping its young people to compete with youngsters from other states. Nobody got terribly excited. Rockefeller—with his fine record in industrial and economic development—leaned hard on his leadership in that field. This issue did help, as did Rockefeller's charge that Arkansas was being run by a political machine, complete with dishonesty at the ballot box. But WR was looking for indignation on the part of the people. He didn't run into much of it, despite his vehemence. There was an attitude of apathy toward Rockefeller's general charges of dishonesty.

But because Rockefeller loyalists strongly felt that their man had literally been cheated at the ballot box, it was hoped that some probing would turn up some odious evidence and, just maybe, the people of Arkansas would finally become incensed about dishonesty at the polls. With this objective in mind, Rockefeller and the Republicans who had been in the front lines of his campaign joined forces again—this time to see if they couldn't pry the lid off and give themselves and the citizenry a good look at just what was there.

County officials and others in Madison County reacted with Hollywood-type "Whatcha doin' here, boy?" responses as they closed ranks to fend off the Republicans, led in this case by John Haley, a Little Rock attorney and a Democrat who directed the Election Research Council. Haley and two Republican cohorts—Joe Gaspard of Fayetteville and Bob Scott of Rogers—were threatened with incarceration and "bodily harm" when they went to Huntsville to check on the absentee ballot situation. One person told Haley in a courthouse office, "Stick around tonight and you might be dead."[8] But for the first time, the Republicans weren't going to be sent packing so easily by scowling deputy sheriffs. Thus, more elaborate preventive measures seemed called for by the Madison County folks. In defiance of Republican demands and the law, they simply refused to let the voting records be copied. One pushy Republican got a well-aimed fist to the head for his pains. The Republicans went to court after three attempts to copy the records were rebuffed by the Madison County clerk and his reinforcements. They got a writ of mandamus (after the case was twice postponed in Madison County Chancery Court) and went back to the clerk, writ in hand, so to speak.

Again they were turned away by the county clerk, who appealed the chancery court ruling. The stubborn Republicans prepared and filed still another suit to get at the records. This time the chancellor (after two more postponements) turned the Republicans down for not supplying sufficient evidence that they had been turned down by the county clerk. Therefore, they put a formal request in writing and got it back to the county clerk; they returned after three days with the idea that finally they might get to copy the records. That's when one of the Republicans was struck in the side of the head when he asked to see the clerk. The Republicans packed their bags and left.

But it wasn't over. Four Republican women, who told reporters they were going to rely on chivalry, headed north to Madison County from Little Rock. They got just about the same treatment as their male predecessors, although perhaps because of chivalry none of the women was actually hit by a county official. Back in Little Rock, the women went to see Faubus. They didn't get an audience. That night, the problem was "solved," more or less. All the voting records disappeared from the Madison County clerk's office. The Republicans offered a reward of $1,000 for information leading to arrest of the thief or thieves.[9]

One newspaper commented editorially that it didn't think the reward was the highest bid offered for those records and didn't look for them "to turn up anytime soon" as a result of that offer. An editorial in the *Arkansas Gazette* summed up the situation this way: "Public records ought—by any rational standard—to be available to copying as well as for inspection. The reason they are public records is so that interested parties can make inquiry into public business. If an election is not public business, nothing is. If Republicans are not interested parties in a general election, no one is." The Republicans went to court again. This time they obtained an injunction against the county officials to prevent them from destroying certain duplicate records. The Madison County folks went on and burned the materials anyway.[10]

The whole incident had an interesting effect on Rockefeller. He had preached against dishonesty and corruption in his 1964 campaign and now—in the period between it and the next election—he really had something to talk about. The theft of some voting records and the burning of

others seemed to validate what he'd been charging all
along, and he used one of his favorite phrases, "by cracky,"
as he appealed to the people's sense of fair play. He thought
he was beginning to detect old-fashioned indignation in
the people, despite the depressing evidence the pollster
kept turning up that folks just weren't all that concerned
about what had been happening. Rockefeller had to believe that the seeds were sown, and he set about watering
the crop with a passion. It appears, in retrospect, that
Rockefeller was correct in his analysis of public opinion,
since Faubus opted not to seek a seventh term when the
time came. There may have been many reasons, but surely
one was that he knew he would have an even tougher time
of it than he'd had in 1964.

Meanwhile, Rockefeller aides were sifting through the
right and wrong things done during the campaign by the
fledgling WR organization. They hoped to avoid repeating
really damaging mistakes.

Faubus had bested Rockefeller on the civil rights issue:
and he also profited from his claims that he was a "poor
boy," that the Rockefeller campaign was obscenely expensive, that Rockefeller had an army of hired employees, that
out-of-state professionals were running the WR campaign.
Equally effective were Faubus' charges that Rockefeller
kept and drank copious amounts of whiskey at Winrock,
that he had been divorced as had his present wife, and that
he was hardly more than a carpetbagger.

Had Faubus made those charges stick? It was a worri-
some question. Faubus had handled them with mastery;
the aides knew that. He had even gained some mileage on
the question of where Rockefeller got his hair cut. And he
had attracted just about everyone's amused attention with
his claim that Rockefeller kept more booze at Winrock
than any Arkansas liquor store. Rockefeller tried to one-up
that attack in a much-publicized television debate between the two men.[11] He said he did keep liquor at Win-

rock and that some of it was "ancient spirits." The whiskey was there for entertaining folks who came to call and look at Arkansas as a possible plant site. In fact, the good governor himself had partaken, Rockefeller said smilingly, with a look at Faubus. The governor smiled back; and the next morning he was shaking his fist and preaching again from the stump about Rockefeller's whiskey—making just as much, if not more, of it as ever. An old issue that had plagued governors in Arkansas before Faubus arrived on the scene was gambling. Rockefeller had tried to make this an issue, pointing out that Faubus had allowed gambling to flourish illegally at Hot Springs and that he only closed it down when Rockefeller put the pressure on. Not many folks thought WR benefited from this strategy. The people really didn't want to think about it.

Why did they vote for Rockefeller—the 43 percent who did? More than half of them voted for him because they felt the need for a change in the governor's office. This need for change was reason enough to cut across all lines—Democrats, Republicans, Independents, white, black, labor, business, regardless of the size of the cities or areas of the state. Few gave political party reasons for voting for Rockefeller, even among Republicans. When given an opportunity to state their reasons without prompting, very few cited the education issue as a basis for supporting Rockefeller. They gave it lip service when asked, but it wasn't really a basis for voting for or against either man.

One could sense certain attitudes in the people during the campaign, but it was difficult to know in specific terms what those attitudes were and how they were distributed. For example, education was mentioned often as a key issue, but in rural Arkansas the top issue was roads. Arkansas was still naturally divided into communities of counties with common interests that varied widely from county to county. And the politician who didn't understand what those interests were in each area, who dealt with the wrong interests in a given locality, found himself talking to yawns and crying babies—unless, of course, that politician was the old spellbinder. Faubus' ability to find common threads uniting everyone's interests was nothing short of genius. He made his appeals to the gut level, and he did it so well that Rockefeller's running mate in 1964—Travis Beeson—introduced WR at a political rally once by exhorting his listeners to go to the polls and "vote with your heart, not your head." Rockefeller said later, with wry humor, that this had been a tough line to follow. He confessed that he had actually wanted to strike Beeson, who remained blithely unaware of what he had said or what it meant.

But that wasn't the only disheartening thing about the campaign of 1964. Rockefeller—trying to build a Republican party—had reason for optimism when the polls showed a decline in Democratic ranks; he hoped the next step would be over into the GOP harness. Not so. After the election, the numbers of Democrats seemed to swell again, back almost to the level held before the campaign; and the Independent category dwindled proportionately. For all practical purposes, things were just about where they had been before Rockefeller began his two-party efforts in 1960.

But the general public thought the GOP was better off than it actually was. They failed to recognize something that Rockefeller's detractors had maintained all along—that it really wasn't a Republican party building at all, but a Rockefeller cult, and that when he was gone, the GOP as any kind of force would be gone as well.

How "Republican" was Rockefeller, anyway?

Some Republicans, Rockefeller said often in 1964, didn't like the idea of his running because they disagreed with his brother Nelson. When people asked him where he stood between Nelson and Goldwater, Rockefeller would say, "That's just what I do. I stand between Nelson and Goldwater."

There were many ways in which Rockefeller was not in agreement with rank-and-file Republicans. His liberal stance on the racial question was a striking example. Rockefeller said at one point in the 1964 campaign that his own views on racial matters were "not vastly different" from those of Governor Faubus—and thus not a valid campaign issue. Although WR's statement was perhaps intentionally vague, what he was trying to say was that Faubus was not nearly so far to the right on that particular issue as many folks thought.

Rockefeller did not try very hard to modify any of his views to accommodate the philosophy of the Republican party in Arkansas. Often, when he tried to compromise, it didn't work out well. For example, when Rockefeller was the guest on NBC's "Meet the Press," the interview ranged over several areas before zeroing in on one that Rockefeller could have bent into a terrific political statement. But his responses fell flat.[12] He was asked about legalizing casino gambling in Arkansas, whether he was for it or opposed to it. The staff members back in Little Rock, with eyes glued to the TV screen, settled back in their chairs, knowing WR would be solid on this one. "I am very much in favor of putting this question before the people. This has been a political football for generations," WR answered. The aides in Little Rock, alarmed, sat up straight again. "But your position, Mr. Rockefeller," the interviewer bore in. "Are you for legalized gambling in Arkansas or against it?" Rockefeller said he was "for letting the people of the state of Arkansas take the position that they want and speak for themselves. This has come up in the legislature time and time again." With some incredulity the interviewer asked, "You don't have an opinion about it?" The stunned staff, by now pacing about in a panic, was equally incredulous. "Yes," Rockefeller finally said. "I have seen nothing about legalized gambling that I think is good. I think morally it is wrong."

He had really wanted to say that all along, but Rockefel-

ler had difficulty communicating. And this problem was
shared by others in WR's organization. Some of his aides,
who in ordinary life were fairly good at conveying their
thoughts to others, sometimes lapsed into vagueness and
obfuscation when working on WR matters. One aide,
Bethel Larey, summarized the problem in a letter in August, 1964:

> Our ad writers, speech writers, etc. must avoid pedantic,
> academic, overly abstract, three-dollar words and sentences.
> Not only do they fail to communicate our story to those we
> haven't convinced, but they convey an impression of being
> condescending, grandiloquent and abstruse. Brother Faubus
> has learned how to mix homely analogies, trite sayings,
> chauvinistic pleas, corny slogans, monstrous lies and bellicose
> tactics into unsurpassed vote-getting speeches.[13]

Faubus could fashion other word images as well. In
1965, before it was clear that the incumbent governor
wouldn't seek a seventh term, he said about Rockefeller,
"It would be a disgrace for him to be governor of Arkansas
or any other state." A writer for a Boston newspaper observed: "By hint and innuendo, Faubus constantly con-
veys the impression that he considers Rockefeller morally
unfit for high office. He never gets more specific than mentioning Rockefeller's divorce or liquor collection."[14]

Rockefeller was burdened with other negatives as he
continued to push his way into the mainstream of Arkansas politics. For one thing, in a still provincial state, he was
an outsider. In September of 1964, I wrote Earl King of the
New York *News* to say, as WR's public relations man, that I
was glad King planned to cover the campaign. "I can't say
that I am happy with the approach you outlined to write
more of a personality piece on one of New York's most illustrious expatriates, rather than on the campaign itself.
Anything that appears in print implying that Mr. Rockefeller is really a New Yorker transplanted into the state will
damage us. Mr. Rockefeller is an Arkansan. He is here for
life, and that's all there is to it."[15]

But it wasn't only New York writers who viewed Arkansas' own Rockefeller as an "illustrious expatriate." Faubus noticed it almost before Rockefeller had unpacked his suitcases. The two men were in Booneville—Rockefeller as the new chairman of the AIDC—to welcome a new industry to the town of 2,700. Some 2,000 people assembled and heard Faubus acknowledge that they had obviously turned out to see Rockefeller, since Faubus himself had only drawn a crowd of 300 on his last visit to Booneville.

But expatriate or not, Rockefeller did not possess any of the brashness Arkansans had come to expect in folks from the North. At least a measure of it would have served him well, many of his admirers sometimes thought as they sat and strained with him while he moved in his own way through a speech. His awkwardness, his shyness before a crowd never left him, even after countless appearances and campaign speeches.

Margaret Kolb, a tough-minded teetotaling Baptist leader who stuck by Rockefeller through everything—even though she strongly disapproved of him on occasion—remembers that he came across in his speeches as a very timid person. "Really, it endeared him to a lot of people. They had been used to the polished, oratorical Southern Democrat type of politician, and it was very refreshing to have a very wealthy man, big in stature, and yet not a good speaker, getting up in front of a crowd. This psychologically appealed, especially to women. They all wanted to mother him."[16]

John Robert Starr, chief of the Associated Press (AP) bureau in Little Rock, commented, "I guess that all poor boys have a built-in prejudice against millionaires. I was favorably impressed by him and thought 'here is a man that really knows what he is doing.' He was not at all what I expected a millionaire to be. It was sometime later that he began to act like one."[17]

Regardless of whether he was "acting like a millionaire," Rockefeller had definite likes and dislikes that extended to a variety of things and people. One thing he disliked was the political situation in Conway County, his home. A newspaperman named Gene Wirges who had taken up residence there was himself extremely displeased with the political set-up, and he and the "man on the mountain" some thirteen miles away were destined to join forces in a largely unsuccessful move to break up what most people called the Conway County machine. Their joining forces would be a disruptive element in the Rockefeller organization, because the Conway County editor was a man you liked or hated with equal passion.

Eisele saw the Wirges-Rockefeller unification as "one of the greatest examples of the man's [Rockefeller's] stand on principles." Eisele said that in his opinion Rockefeller never liked Wirges as a person, but worked with him anyway because they believed in the same cause. Eisele's portrayal of the situation in Conway County when Rockefeller and Wirges entered the picture was as follows: "Here was an abuse of state power by the local politicians, the local people. They were using the courts. They were using the legal process. They were using their political power, and the power of the state to silence an opposition editor up there. This man [Rockefeller] spent Lord only knows how much to prevent them from doing it."[18]

The courts slapped all kinds of judgments on Wirges, but every case was reversed. "You don't pick your heroes," Eisele said, explaining that Rockefeller was not pleased with Wirges' style, his way of seeking to bring about change, though he supported Wirges in the effort because of the principle involved. Everett Ham brought the Wirges matter to Rockefeller's attention. Ham would later be jailed—along with Marion Burton—in connection with the political fight. "I really got involved with Gene when they [the anti-Wirges faction] were going to sell his paper [the Morrilton *Democrat*]," Ham recalled. "I took it upon myself to be the savior of it, so I called WR one night and said they were going to sell it the next day and I said, 'What can I do?' Win didn't want to be directly concerned with it, so he said, 'Everett, if you will get somebody to do it I will stand behind it.' I got old Doctor Gutowski [the late Stanley Gutowski, a Perry County physician and a strong Republican]. Doc had enough confidence in me to go down to the bank before it opened, get the money and go over and pay it off."[19] The amount needed to prevent foreclosure was something over $11,000. That would be but the first drop in the bucket. Wirges editorialized extensively against Sheriff Marlin Hawkins and others in county and Morrilton city government, and he was sued repeatedly. He was beaten up once on the streets of Morrilton by W. O. "Bus" Hice, a county official. Finally, his wife Betty became the editor, after legal moves by the opposition forced that on them; and their fight against Hawkins and the others continued. (For a brief time, a company owned mainly by Rockefeller—Transportation Properties, Inc.— owned the newspaper, even though owning newspapers or publishing companies was against family policy.)

Meanwhile, Faubus was trying to stay out of the Conway County mess as much as he could, though he was sympathetic to the Hawkins side. Instead, the governor was busily spending his time polishing 1964 campaign phrases like this one: "I remember how hard it was when I was a boy and old man John D. Rockefeller raised the price of coal oil a penny. It was my job to stick a sweet potato on the spout of the jug to keep it from spilling out, because at the prices the Rockefellers charged, we couldn't afford to spill a drop." Rockefeller wondered if Faubus' preoccupation with the price of coal oil in 1911 was effective. The staff tried to reassure him that it wasn't, but they were never really sure. It did portray one of Faubus' main themes— that Rockefeller didn't understand the problems of the common man because he had never been one. Rockefeller tried to counter by wondering if, having broken your leg, you would be wise to leave it unset until you found a doctor who had suffered a broken leg himself to set yours for you. It was a pretty good line, but Rockefeller simply couldn't grind it across convincingly.

In fact, his speaking ability was often the subject of analytical pieces in newspapers and magazines; there were items on conversations between WR and voters who rarely got the message Rockefeller was trying to communicate to them, except that they noticed his nervousness. Bill Lewis, writing in the *Arkansas Gazette*, commented on one aspect of Rockefeller's speaking ability: "Rockefeller's stump humor is ponderous at best, and it often misfires. Not infrequently, he makes certain that his audience knows that he's going to tell them a witticism, for he will say something like 'And now for a bit of levity.' The best laughs are those that follow a well-rehearsed punch line, and on occasion Rockefeller will change them and in so doing, remove the punch."[20]

Yet humor seemed the best defense against the kind of campaign Faubus was mounting. Faubus played the issue of Rockefeller's appreciation for beverage alcohol to the fullest. In a television address in July, 1964, he promised solemnly, "So long as I am governor, the executive mansion will not become the scene of drinking parties and the guest houses will not become the headquarters of beatniks from other states."[21]

A headline on a flyer issued on behalf of Faubus in the 1964 campaign read: "Winthrop Rockefeller, the multimillionaire still has to go back to New York to get his hair cut." The flyer portrayed Rockefeller with a neat haircut beside newspaper handouts with various excerpts indicating that Rockefeller flew from coast to coast in his own jet airplane, which cost $750,000, and that he bought and sold expensive cattle, costing as much as $50,000 each. The flyer was signed by an otherwise unidentified person who offered this comment: "My yearly income is roughly $6,000. I drive a $2,500 automobile 16 miles to my barber for haircuts." This was just another variation on the "Rockefeller isn't one of us" theme.[22]

Faubus was a master at hurling a charge and then repeating it while his opponent floundered around trying to refute the charge. The governor began to say that Rockefeller owned an interest in a gambling casino in Puerto Rico.[23] This charge was vaguely related to the fact that WR's brother Laurance did own properties in the Puerto Rico area, including the Dorado Beach Hotel, which contained a gambling casino. Rockefeller indignantly denied that he had any interest in the hotel or any other facility that offered gambling, and Faubus responded that he had been led to believe the family (including WR, of course) owned the property. The next day, however, Faubus was back on the stump, saying exactly the same thing, that Rockefeller owned an interest in a gambling casino.

It became apparent to Rockefeller and his staff that they lacked the political expertise necessary to win battles with Faubus on moral issues. Early in the campaign, WR tried to carry on such a fight and he elicited a response that was overwhelming because of its completeness and passion. His staff raised the moral issue with a letter from campaign headquarters implying strongly that Faubus was not the one who ought to be moralizing; the response was a letter mailed all over the state from Corbett Mask, a Benton minister. Mask's letter said: "Whatever our faith, whatever our denomination, we instinctively rebel at the prostitution of the Christian religion."[24] Enclosed with Mask's letter was a copy of an affidavit about the stock of liquor Rockefeller had brought to Arkansas in 1953, a newspaper story about Rockefeller's having failed to pay proper tax on it, and a newspaper story showing bars and drinking activity at Winrock. The letter concluded with this question: "Has Rockefeller earned the right to challenge Governor Faubus on moral issues? I think not."

Another item included in Mask's mailing was a reprint of an article that had been published in May in the Pine Bluff *Commercial*, a feature story on a Winrock cattle sale. The article contained statements like: "Those who did manage to tear themselves away from their cocktails were chauffeured in Winrock Farms cars to the food tent, which was located near the stable and sales arena."

Rockefeller could take only so much personal abuse. Finally, in an appearance in late October, 1964, before the Little Rock Ministerial Alliance, he laid it on Faubus "pretty hard," in Faubus' words. Rockefeller opened his remarks to the ministers by describing the campaign a bit, listing the reasons he was in the race, citing his background and the religious interests of his parents and grandparents. He talked about his family traditions and the fact that the tradition of service was one he was trying to continue in Arkansas, but he admitted to being a neophyte in the field of politics. Then he launched into his attack:

> I did not anticipate the sordid, sinister tactics which I have encountered. The opposition has instigated a campaign of slander, smears and tears, a campaign of suspicion, fear, cynicism, greed and arrogance. I am deeply concerned as I know you are. All citizens must similarly be wondering why the desperate but deliberate and callous attempt at character assassination has been directed towards me in this campaign. My opponent, who in 1957 signed a legislative resolution commending me for my leadership in connection with the Arkansas Industrial Development Commission says of me today "Untried, inexperienced, former playboy. He wants to be governor simply because he has the whim, the time and the money." He says further, "I must now destroy the false image of Winthrop Rockefeller that I helped to create."
>
> Gentlemen, I have not sought to create an image. I have been myself and my life has been an open book. As a matter of fact, with the name of Rockefeller I have felt, on occasion, it was almost too open! I have not been perfect. Which of us has? My opponent has been concerned and made a campaign issue of

the price of coal oil in 1911, while I have been trying to make an issue of the educational needs of the youth of our state. My opponent has been trying to make an issue of eating a can of chili while I have been trying to make an issue of the needs of our worthy welfare recipients. My opponent has been trying to make an issue of riding a freight train while I have been trying to make an issue of improving the highway system in Arkansas.

Rockefeller continued in this vein, stabbing in near the end with, "My opponent has been trying to make an issue of where I get my hair cut while I have been trying to make an issue of the fiscal integrity of the state's administration."[25]

As Rockefeller was making this uncharacteristic attack, Faubus sat in surprised silence. But Rockefeller would get even stronger. He said there had been injected into the campaign "a flow of tragically warped, insinuating and sometimes disgusting materials in the mails and by word of mouth. All of this, however, does not seem to be enough, for most recently, my opponent dropped to an all-time low as quoted in the *Northwest Arkansas Times* on October 23, 'Orval Faubus added a new charge to his list against Winthrop Rockefeller, cemetery wrecker.' The story continued 'If Rockefeller is so kindhearted, why did he level this cemetery without regard to the feelings of the relatives or respect for the dead?' In this attack he was appealing to the most sensitive of human feelings. The fact that the story is a complete fabrication," Rockefeller continued passionately, "a lie, and has been denied, makes little difference. It has been said. The damage has been done."[26]

Faubus offered his own surprise at this ministerial meeting. He made a speech that was clear of politics, until he asserted, near the end of his speech, that "a political candidate should meet the qualifications of a Baptist deacon." Faubus said the candidate should "have one wife and not love whiskey."

That was the cue, so to speak, for M. L. Moser, Jr., a close ally of Faubus and a Little Rock minister, to ask Rockefeller if his wife had been divorced and if he had been divorced. Since Moser wasn't even a member of the organization, Rockefeller concluded that he was there just to ask those questions. Later in the day the executive secretary of the Arkansas Council of Churches and a member of the alliance issued a statement that Moser was not a member and that his question had no place in the political campaign. But again, the damage was done.

The "cemetery wrecker" issue evinced an overly sensitive response from an aghast Rockefeller and was credited by many with sinking him. In a special television address two or three weeks before the end of the campaign, Faubus appeared waving photographs and charging that Rockefeller had bulldozed down a cemetery as a part of his farm near Carlisle, in blatant, callous disregard for the sentiments of the people whose relatives were buried there. "After he went in there and bulldozed around and so on, he made a feeble attempt to pick up a few of the stones and put a fence around it," Faubus charged. He left the impression that Rockefeller had simply bulldozed the cemetery to make more pasture for his cows to graze; then, when it was feared neighbors might complain at such callousness, he had hastily and clumsily attempted to "cover up" the desecration.[27]

The facts are that a bulldozer operator under contract to clear portions of the farm did in fact accidentally run into the cemetery, which was overgrown from years of neglect. When he saw what he had done, he backed out and the stones that had been knocked over were re-erected. Then a fence was put around the area, fencing it "out" of the farm, and thus making it accessible to visitors (should any want to come) and not accessible from the farm. From the looks of it, had Faubus not raised the issue, Robinson Cemetery would have continued to attract virtually no visitors, except the birds and small animals finding haven in the dense undergrowth. But with Faubus waving photographs and railing against Rockefeller, the cemetery drew more attention in a few days than it apparently had in the previous twenty years, especially from newsmen and photographers, of course.[28]

In the course of events that followed, Rockefeller got a letter[29] from one individual who claimed to have relatives in the cemetery, suggesting that to make amends Rockefeller should construct an elaborate concrete depiction of angels and other creatures in a religious scene. It was such an incredible project as described in the letter that one of WR's lawyer friends suggested that he build the thing just as the writer dictated, to prove once and for all the idiocy of the whole thing. But even though some laughed at the ridiculous charge, Rockefeller was not amused. He reacted sensitively and keenly, as perhaps Faubus knew he would. Because of his uncommon respect for family and ancestry, WR believed that a presentation of the facts had to be made. Several members of his staff did not agree, but their objections were voiced feebly. No one, after all, wanted to take responsibility for not doing something and thereby losing the campaign.

Thus it was agreed that Rockefeller and some others would go on television to "prove" his innocence. The title for the Rockefeller program was "Here Lies Orval Faubus," a pun lost on most viewers. Rockefeller sent teams of aides, photographers, and others to Carlisle to get the story, and an elaborate presentation was prepared to refute the charge. Meanwhile, Faubus was out in the boondocks gleefully pounding away at this sensitive nerve he had exposed. He had found a super way to show Rockefeller as a callous millionaire who cared nothing about the concerns of the "little man." Rockefeller's TV show response was a political blunder, no question about it.

Faubus said years later that he didn't think WR's cemetery response was a major factor in his defeat. With an issue like that, he explained, one side says it is all true and the other side says it is all false, and then the people are forced to make a decision. Faubus wasn't condemning Rockefeller, he said. "It could happen to any rich man that had all this property and couldn't look after it personally. You can charge any rich man under the sun with that, because he can't look after all the things." But asked whether the charge was true, whether Rockefeller did desecrate a cemetery, Faubus answered: "I'm convinced that it was partial truth at least, maybe completely. But I am also of the opinion that Mr. Rockefeller didn't know anything about it."[30] Maybe this was one of the reasons a frustrated and angry Rockefeller once remarked that trying to beat Faubus was "like trying to fight a marshmallow."

It would have helped if Rockefeller had been blessed with a top-notch organization in 1964. He wasn't. His campaign opening of his state headquarters in Little Rock was a hectic affair, and it got off to a memorable start that was to characterize the whole campaign. Rockefeller was driven out to the airport—his airport—atop Petit Jean Mountain for the short flight to the capital city. He had four airplanes at the time, including a jet, and they served his personal needs as well as those of Winrock Farms. When the big maroon Lincoln bearing the candidate pulled up at the airport, the one airport handyman did a considerable amount of whitefaced scurrying around. Finally, the man got on the intercom and hailed down a plane that happened to be in the area, and Rockefeller chartered it on the spot to convey him to Little Rock. He took the whole incident in good humor, but a more precise accounting about which planes were where and why was inaugurated the very next day by farm staff.

This is not to say the campaign was a comedy of errors. Far from it. There were many solid blocks on which the next campaign, the winning one, was built. One of those was the "Statement of Beliefs" Rockefeller adapted from his father's statement of years before.[31] This declaration of sixteen principles proved the most successful campaign document Rockefeller distributed through all the campaigns, and it may have been the most widely circulated campaign document in Arkansas political history.

But with this and other touchstones of solidity, there were the confusing things as well. Ham said he called over to the headquarters one day and asked for the campaign manager, Eisele. The switchboard operator told Ham there was no one there by that name. Ham went into apoplexy, and he wasn't calmed by being told that it was a "new girl" who had never heard of Eisele. The fact is, Eisele rarely went to the headquarters, and the girl had been on the job for some time without having met Eisele.

Rockefeller had some good issues to work with, to compensate in part for the inexperience of his campaign organization. His strongest, of course, was that Faubus was the head cog in an insidious political machine that was choking the life out of Arkansas. And Rockefeller said it all over Arkansas. He traveled the state in a campaign that surprised even those close to him for its vigor, and he tried not to lose his sense of humor, even when he was vexed beyond belief.

Rockefeller recalled telephoning Eisele in the middle of the night once:

> The temperature was running about 106 daily. I was making five and six stops a day. I went to the dedication of the airport at Mount Ida. We had five or six stops, ending up in Conway that night. Tom, with his typical enthusiasm and bounciness, said, "Well, if you'd get on the road by 9 o'clock, we could work in one more picnic during the day." I was angered, and as I remember, we didn't schedule the additional 9 o'clock junket. But we left at 10 A.M. and got back to Winrock at 8 P.M. and then had to go to Conway. We changed pilots because we had been going all day long. We didn't even have time to eat supper. The other people supposed to take part in the program at Con-

way didn't show, so the rodeo officials kept running in other little duties for me. What I had agreed to do at 3 P.M. was finally done at 1 in the morning. We got back to Winrock just flat punchy, and when you get punchy, you get giggly. We came to the conclusion that since the second crew of pilots had only been out six hours, we had two more hours to go. So we called Tom, woke him up and asked where to next? But I don't think his sense of humor totally rose to the occasion. His reaction was, "Well, there's only one Fourth of July each year."[32]

Rockefeller's speeches in those 1964 outings were attempts at emphasis on the positive, though he enjoyed needling his opponent without plunging into name-calling or the more serious, though typical of Arkansas politics, character assassinations. In a characteristic speech in eastern Arkansas WR inquired of his listeners: "Has Orval Faubus been here yet? Because, mark well, when he does, he'll be in the courthouse over there greasing his machine and you go over there and tell him to come out and speak to the people."

Faubus had his own unique campaign style. Driving to Rison in southern Arkansas to a speech-making, he passed a team of mules hauling three big logs to a mill. The wagon was driven by a black man. The governor commented, as they drove on past the cars of newsmen dutifully following along in the entourage, that he had driven mules as a young man while working in timber. His publicity man, Bob Troutt, went to work. The car and then the caravan were halted. The governor was taken back to the wagon, accompanied by press and television crewmen. He climbed up on the wagon seat and clucked to the team of mules. They started to trot, and the wagon careened down a hill. Faubus and everyone else was frightened. He got them stopped, climbed out of the wagon, and observed to no one in particular that the wagon didn't have any brakes. "I noticed that when I got on it, but back where I lived in the hills all the wagons had to have brakes or they wouldn't have made it."

Rockefeller wasn't going to be outclassed by that. He found occasion to comment that Faubus was trying to keep Arkansas in the mule-drawn wagon era while he was trying to move the state into the jet age. But the stunt was effective—once again dramatizing that Faubus was "one of the people" and Rockefeller merely an interloper from New York. Rockefeller later found an opportunity to drive a team of mules himself during a parade. The mules were given tranquilizers before he took the reins, though WR knew how to handle a team pretty well and the precaution probably wasn't necessary.

For all Rockefeller's honest lack of political experience, Faubus viewed him as a serious threat in 1964. "I always thought I was a fairly good political analyst. At the time Rockefeller ran against me, I viewed him as the most serious threat I had faced. The difficulty was convincing my friends that he was a serious threat." Faubus said he wasn't behind at any point, but he got "stuck on 48 percent for a long time." At one time in the campaign, Rockefeller and Faubus were locked up at 46 percent each, which left 8 percent undecided. Faubus said those figures held for about two or three weeks. That's when he got out on the stump and made a super effort to enlist the support of the people all over Arkansas. It worked.

On election night, in his plush office where he seemed most at home, Rockefeller was—as usual—surrounded by lots of aides and other people. He had a drink in his hand, and it was a familiar, comfortable situation all around, except for one thing: He had lost.

Rockefeller was now trim, tanned, and tough, and he had wanted the office of governor very much—maybe as much as anything he had ever wanted. Wanting it and working for it had been a tonic for WR. Even in losing, you could see it. His campaign-sharpened wit and spirit didn't flag. He was inspiring on election night. He knew he had done a lot, maybe a lot more than even his close friends thought him capable of. So what was it all for? Orval E.

Faubus had beaten him, hadn't he? On the surface it all seemed simple enough; but inside, the complex Rockefeller was evaluating, reacting, forming plans as ingenious as they might be unworkable, rationalizing the loss somewhat. This was nothing more than an expected first step toward victory, he said encouragingly. But somehow you had the feeling that maybe along toward the end there he had thought he was going to win.

At any rate, he had gone further into this effort personally than anything before. And even though Arkansas seemed unyielding to his customary approach to getting what he wanted, WR would have the governor's office. For him there was no way back. There was agreement on both sides of the fence that his time would come, indeed was here. Rockefeller could wait, but not long.

He sent Faubus a telegram: "Congratulations on your victory. I know you are gratified, as I am, in the splendid increase in voter participation in the election process. I pledge my continued efforts on behalf of a better Arkansas."[33] Faubus later expressed his belief in the importance of timing, and he said Rockefeller "came at a time when the situation was right."[34]

CHAPTER III

The First
Victory

Rockefeller—having garnered more than twice as many votes as any Republican had previously—was not embarrassed by his 1964 defeat. He was looking forward to 1966 and a chance to take on the old master again. He would win; he could feel it in his bones.

But there was an enemy out there more formidable even than Orval Faubus—an enemy that would hinder Rockefeller in just about any of the things he wanted to accomplish. It was disinterest, inertia. It plagued the electorate like nothing Rockefeller had seen before, and all his finger-stabbing speeches about his dream of an indignant public throwing rascals out of office and raising hell about bad government were not getting folks stirred up.

In late 1965 the public's favorable and unfavorable ratings of Rockefeller were essentially unchanged from those of the previous year. Those unchanged ratings had to be disappointing, what with Rockefeller preparing for another campaign against Faubus. As a matter of fact, for all of WR's preaching about Faubus' shortcomings, the incumbent governor had enjoyed a small but significant increase in favorable ratings. But despite these discouraging reports, Rockefeller was determined to run against, and this time defeat, Orval Faubus. Faubus—with 71 percent favorable November, 1965, ratings—would be the man to beat, Rockefeller and most of his aides believed. Faubus appeared to be the first choice of the people as the best Democratic candidate to face Rockefeller. The second choice was Senator John L. McClellan. Jim Johnson didn't show.

The survey of opinion in late 1965 confirmed once more a depressing fact. The Republican party still wasn't growing—not at all. The 11 percent was precisely the same as in 1961. Something else would have to be done, if the percentage was to be upped at all. However, with the breakdown of yellow-dog Democrat voting patterns, Rockefeller could win without a majority of hardcore Republicans. The objective, no matter how privately distasteful to loyal Republicans, was to woo Democrats and Independents without driving away the Republicans already in the fold. More than 60 percent of the people felt the Republican party had gained strength (even though it hadn't) and that this augured well for the GOP. This change in public opinion seemed to increase the social acceptability of individuals identifying themselves as Republicans. But did it? No such acceptability was evident in the growth in party ranks.

Three issues were most on the minds of the people of Arkansas.[1] Assuming that the people voted for candidates on the basis of issues, it seemed critically important to define the public's desires exactly and to map plans for satisfying those desires. Education was the primary issue. Roads and highways were the second-most important category. And the third was employment. Most voters thought that education ought to be improved, with vocational education and senior high schools leading the list in educational concerns. There was also, of course, substantial support for improvement of all public schools and for the introduction of public kindergartens. Specific areas for educational improvement included better pay for teachers, more schoolrooms, free textbooks, and better curricula.

The only problem with all these areas of progress urged by the people was a correspondingly strong feeling that not another cent of taxes should be exacted from them. The obvious paradox here may have escaped the people, but it didn't get past Rockefeller. As an honest man, he could never see—even when his aides repeatedly explained it to him—how a man could stump the state promising the improvements the public desired without telling them how he proposed to pay for these improvements. WR would, in spite of contrary advice, propose tax increases and bond issues to finance needed improvements. And even though the people never enthusiastically supported him in these revenue-producing programs, he did break down some of their resistance by constantly showing them the hypocrisy of candidates promising services without proposing any means for funding them. WR's successor would benefit from his courageous talk of taxes and bond issues.

By late 1965, the polls indicated that people thought it would be a bad idea for Faubus to seek a seventh term— partly because they felt fourteen years was too long for anyone to be governor and partly because they felt Faubus' "political machine" needed breaking up. Some just felt a change was needed. Yet an effort to evoke indignation in the people, over election irregularities and misuse of office by Faubus, produced slim hopes that a fire could be built under either of these potentially emotional issues.

Once it was clear that Faubus was out of the race, Rockefeller tried to shift his strategy so as not to lose all the data-gathering and orientation efforts of his campaign organization. In a speech to a Republican fund-raising dinner in Huntsville, Faubus' hometown, Rockefeller said, "It doesn't make any difference who my opponent will be, because we are not running against an individual and never have. We are running against a machine, and the individual candidate who survives the Democratic primary and runoff will be the machine candidate. Therefore, my fight in November can be portrayed quite simply as 'man against machine.' "[2]

By May of 1966, the hopes of the Rockefeller organization—that their man was stronger than ever politically and had the inside track on the governor's chair—were fading somewhat. A series of trial heats matching Rockefeller with various Democrats had not been encouraging.[3] Dale Alford beat WR 49 to 38; Sam Boyce was almost even, 41 to WR's 42 percent; Brooks Hays had a comfortable margin, 48 to 35; Frank Holt had 49 to 36; and Jim Johnson had 46 percent to WR's 37. There were other candidates, and their strength relative to WR's was equally disconcerting. Had the wheels come off the Rockefeller campaign machine? The race was going to be very, very tough. The staff thought WR should have stomped any of these guys; but there they were, right up there with him and, in several cases, ahead.

Any thoughts by Republicans that this would be a party-building year would be shot down by a worried staff of campaign aides who thought they had ample evidence that to try to project Rockefeller as "Mr. Republican" would be political disaster. They made a pact to play the GOP down at every opportunity, while trying to keep the hard-core Republicans from throwing up their hands in disgust. The aides knew that if the issue were ever drawn as Republican versus Democrat their man was doomed. These men didn't earn their preliminary majorities or pluralities over Rockefeller; they held those enviable positions because they were Democrats—put there by the same people who, when asked what they disliked about Rockefeller, listed all kinds of things, with about a third of those reasons being "he is a Republican."

Thus, in May of that election year, 58 percent of the people still considered themselves Democrats, 29 percent claimed to be Independents, and the Republican party's grassroots strength had dwindled to 8 percent.[4] The most devoted Rockefeller followers had to strain a bit to rationalize a victory on the basis of these findings. They watched anxiously as Jim Johnson took off in his primary campaign on a path that hinted more than broadly that he was a courageous, Christian man. He declared war on Lyndon

Johnson's Great Society and several other targets—including a number of Faubus' friends, as well as his opponents for the Democratic nomination.

Dr. Dale Alford, a Little Rock ophthalmologist who had served two terms in Congress after defeating Brooks Hays in a write-in campaign during the racial strife in Little Rock, earned the moniker "Specs Peddler" from Johnson. Frank Holt, a rather low-key Little Rock attorney and supreme court justice, became a "pleasant vegetable" in Johnson's lexicon of political names. And for Hays—who had tried to mediate the controversy between Faubus and President Eisenhower over Central High School—Johnson had a three-worder, "that old quisling."

When Johnson won the primary runoff, the Democratic party hierarchy and a long list of others, including the news media, seemed quite surprised. There were charges, never formally aired, that Rockefeller had manipulated the Democratic primary by getting thousands of his supporters to vote for Johnson because he would be the easiest for Rockefeller to defeat in November. It didn't happen. The Rockefeller organization wasn't strong enough to put together such a campaign as that, even if the team had been certain that it would have been good strategy—and they couldn't agree that it was.

While Johnson was struggling with primary opposition, Rockefeller was facing his own, though the Republican opposition was viewed mostly as a joke. An old Faubus supporter named Gus McMillan had filed against Rockefeller at the last minute, declaring that since he was a country boy with no telephone, anyone who needed to get in touch with him could do so through the Grant County sheriff. Not long afterward, the GOP newspaper headlined a claim that McMillan had offered to pull out of the campaign for a large sum of money. More than a page of the newspaper carried a transcript of a conversation between McMillan and Truman Altenbaumer, the GOP's executive director. Altenbaumer had hidden a tape recorder in his office in anticipation of McMillan's visit. McMillan got 310 votes out of 19,956 cast in the GOP primary.

Meanwhile, Johnson was seeking to create a campaign rhetoric that portrayed Rockefeller as a sort of foreign dictator type who was in Arkansas for what he could get out of it. "Instead of a two-party system," Johnson said in his acceptance speech to the Democratic state convention, "this clever manipulator really wants not a two-party system but a one-man rule in Arkansas."[5] But Johnson was in something of a dilemma, and he knew it. If he called on the strength of Faubus' followers, he was sure to bring down the attack against the old guard that Rockefeller had been chafing to use. On the other hand, could Johnson win without it?

In August, with Johnson's primary victory just past, another assessment of Rockefeller's strength was made, and there was considerable breath-holding among Rockefeller's people. How strong was the white racist vote? Was Johnson viewed as a Democrat? Would he get enough money to run a strong race?

The survey results were encouraging.[6] A trial heat showed Johnson with 45 percent and Rockefeller with 42 percent; 13 percent remained undecided. The fact that the interviews were conducted shortly after the August 9 runoff, at a time when Johnson was still traveling on election momentum, was considered even more encouraging. And it was not hard to believe that Rockefeller could take more than half the undecided voters, since his strength was greater among those who did not vote in the runoff but who planned to vote in the general election.

In the first strong hint of an attitude change among the people—one that would become more obvious in the next few years—a plurality felt that Arkansas was better off now in terms of racial integration (even with a great deal more of it as a fact of life), and a plurality also believed that

Rockefeller would handle the racial situation better than Johnson. This finding could mean only one thing—the day of the clenched fist, "Never!" and schoolhouse-door stands was over, as far as the people of Arkansas were concerned. They might not be all that keen on integration, but they preferred it to strife.

Another significant fact revealed in this survey was that Rockefeller's strength was much greater in the cities and towns than Johnson's. Therefore, a campaign could be concentrated on television and other media. Equally helpful was the fact that these urban voters with the potential for electing Rockefeller could easily be reached by air. WR wouldn't have to repeat his 1964 campaign trips to the boondocks. He could lay it on heavy on the tube and hop from airport to airport, in a sense. He did more than that, of course; but this poll did seem to recommend a different style campaign, one that Rockefeller was only too happy to adopt.

The black vote was going to be significant. Johnson didn't seem to have a prayer with them, and Rockefeller didn't think he'd lose many white votes by making an all-out appeal for black support. The strong segregationists, who would be turned off by WR's catering to blacks, weren't going to be for him anyway. In August, 1966, some 77 percent of the blacks were for Rockefeller; 12 percent for Johnson. It was probably safe to assume that the 12 percent really didn't know who Johnson was. But Rockefeller would tell them.

Pollster Gene Newsom urged Rockefeller to continue taking a moderate, even-tempered, positive approach. This stance would keep him in character, it would intensify his appeal to those with better than an average education, and it just might provoke Johnson into coming out of his corner—carping and slashing, campaigning as he liked to, across the grain. Rockefeller would seek to cut the ground from under Johnson.

WR contemplated making a brief statewide television appearance to set forth what had been bad and good about the Faubus administration—particularly what had been good, along with some suggested changes. Throwing a bouquet or two toward Faubus sounded like the worst possible idea to some of the Rockefeller insiders; but such an approach, given hindsight, would have been helpful, considered solely in terms of politics. There was a reservoir of sentimentally pro-Faubus people whom Johnson had rebuffed. Rockefeller could have acquired some of these voters without endangering his position at all. And it was assumed, even at this early date, that Johnson would attempt to "belly up" to the Faubus forces he had alienated during the primary campaigns. Johnson's runoff rival was Holt; and the winning strategy was to hang Faubus around Holt's neck—portraying him as the "machine" candidate and Faubus' handpicked successor. But of course this strategy, successful against Holt, would not work against Rockefeller. No one was going to say Faubus put Rockefeller in the race!

Johnson had an amazing ability to communicate, an evangelistic delivery that was most effective. The Rockefeller organization could see what kind of campaign was in the making, from the very beginning. Some questions needed answering. How would the people respond to the church membership issue? What were their feelings on the subject of divorce? Which candidate did they think would project the better national image for Arkansas? WR's staff began to research these issues in August, 1966.[7]

Rockefeller had been to church only a few times since he had come to Arkansas, and he was a member of no church in the state. Johnson, on the other hand, claimed regular attendance. When asked if it would make a difference to the people whether the candidate of their choice went to church regularly, 65 percent said it would and 28 percent said it wouldn't. The others had no opinion. Those raw figures, frightening as they were, needed cautious interpretation. The implication to each person interviewed was that the question related to his own church, not just any church. As Newsom commented in his poll report, had the public been asked in succession about a Baptist church, a Catholic church, a synagogue, and a Moslem mosque, the results would have been different.

Rockefeller had been divorced. In 1964 Faubus had successfully used that fact, though he would later be divorced himself, and go on to lose an election, for that matter. When the public was asked: "How about divorce: would you be more inclined or less inclined to vote for a candidate who had been divorced, or would it make any difference?" an amazing (to the Rockefeller people) 74 percent said it would make no difference; only 19 percent said they'd be less inclined to vote for a divorced man.

Who—Rockefeller or Johnson—would make Arkansas look better in the eyes of the nation? The hopes of the WR camp were realized when 59 percent answered "Rockefeller" and 22 percent thought Johnson the better man in this area. Of course injecting any suggestions along this line into the campaign would be risky, assuming that tens of thousands might respond with the eyes-of-the-nation-be-damned theory of "Let them run their business and we'll run ours."

A month after this poll, Rockefeller and Johnson were just about neck and neck in terms of public opinion. It hadn't really moved a peg, if you looked at the raw figures; but a slight movement of opinion in favor of Rockefeller could be measured in terms of the intensity of feeling behind each candidate. Rockefeller's supporters felt more strongly about him. Both men had lost a little, but Johnson had lost more than Rockefeller. Rockefeller was still regarded as better able than Johnson to "handle the racial situation."

In late September, the two men were still running close,

with Rockefeller enjoying increased intensity of partisanship among his supporters. Blacks were for him solidly,
three-to-one. Johnson had lost some black and some white
support when he refused to shake hands with a group of
blacks on the campaign trail, since two out of three Arkansas voters considered keeping the peace on the racial front
of primary importance and contesting federal guidelines
for desegregation secondary. Also, Johnson had called
Rockefeller a "prissy sissy" on a television program, and 90
percent of the people who saw the program were offended
by the remark.

Adding it all up, the picture was heartening for the
Rockefeller camp. There was absolutely no room for com-
placency, Newsom warned; but barring a major fluke or a
racial disturbance, it looked as if Rockefeller might win.
Johnson—no matter which way he turned or what he
did—was gambling, because the opinion structure supporting him was not solid. Any move he made might very
well lose him more than it gained. Rockefeller's support,
more stable, seemed likely to weather anything Johnson
could throw at it.

Questions touching on the racial issue seemed significant at the time. When the people were asked, "Would
you like to see the next governor of Arkansas fight the
guidelines with all forces at his command or challenge the
guidelines through the courts or strive mainly to keep
things as orderly as possible?"—11 percent wanted to
"fight with all forces," 18 percent favored challenging the
courts, 5 percent had no opinion, and 66 percent wanted
the next governor to "keep things as orderly as possible."
Clearly, racial demagoguery was on the down side of opinion for the first time since 1957.

It seemed fitting, in late October, for Rockefeller to present a recapitulation of his program in a manner that
would sum him up and bring him into sharper focus as he
moved into the final days of the campaign. His image was

still somewhat fragmented. Everybody—the field staff, the phalanx around the candidate, the public—was frustrated and confused by WR's difficult expressions, his seemingly grandiose ideas, his troublesome penchant for answering a simple political question with a great plan.

Hot Springs offers a perfect example of this "great plan" approach. Rockefeller had played a major role in forcing the closure of illegal gambling there, by constantly reminding everyone of Governor Faubus' inability to notice the flagrant violation of law. WR knew that many in Hot Springs were turned off by his interference into what they insisted was a "local" matter, but he needed support there. So he conceived a plan, and a grand one it was. He proposed a new Hot Springs to replace the old one that had been so popular with the townspeople, the gamblers, thousands of tourists who invested sizable amounts of their vacation money in illegal mixed drinks and illegal action at the tables. WR's new Hot Springs included a Tivoli, a monorail, a renovated downtown to get rid of the ugly signs, and a coordinated "Ozark Way" (which in fact meant a $200 million redevelopment of Highway 7 through the mountains).[8] The astronomical price tag on all this defied comprehension, even though Rockefeller tried unsuccessfully to convince the people that he was merely presenting a concept, not a firm proposal, as a beginning point for some serious thinking about the future of Hot Springs and all of Arkansas.

"Trolley car in the sky" was the way Jim Johnson scathingly referred to the WR plan. Such an appellation as that would have destroyed the idea, had it had a chance in the first place. The people in Hot Springs were politely interested, but it is doubtful that any of them voted on the basis of it. This plan was typical of Rockefeller's frequently nonspecific, complex style of communication.

Rockefeller could be quite specific, however. In a campaign speech in Pine Bluff, with his craw full of what he considered the self-serving independence of the state highway commission, Rockefeller threatened to fire the whole crew if he were elected governor. Legally, he couldn't do that, because the Mack-Blackwell Amendment to the state constitution separated the commission from such direct control by the governor's office. And in principle, Rockefeller really favored the amendment; in fact, he later appointed Lawrence Blackwell to the commission. WR never said so, but aides knew he regretted his highway commission statement. At any rate, Johnson branded it "asinine" and many agreed with him, including most of the Rockefeller organization. But Johnson had gotten off on tangents of his own that didn't particularly appeal to the people.

By the first of November, with everything more or less locked on course, win or lose, it seemed clear that the Rockefeller campaign was holding up. Some even felt that WR could win big. The two candidates seemed to be running evenly in the rural areas, but Rockefeller still had a strong lead in the larger towns and cities.

Among blacks, the really critical element in the election, Rockefeller was winning hands down. He had come a long way from that day when he admitted that he was actually bewildered to learn that Johnson would be his opponent. "I could not see from the program he had set forth that he really had anything to offer as a candidate," Rockefeller said; and that was why Johnson's nomination had precipitated some major alterations in campaign strategy.

A vignette in the Pine Bluff *Commercial* of October 5, 1966, shows the Jim Johnson that Rockefeller faced:

> John Reese, of North Little Rock, Johnson's driver and aide, leaned against his new car and waited for his candidate to finish his Sheridan politicking. The back seat of the car was filled with clothes and boxes of stickers and buttons. The trunk was full of food—a plastic cooler packed with Cokes, ham, cheese, mayonnaise, honey and milk. In the corner was a large

bottle of high protein supplement. Reese said Johnson drank honey and milk mixed together for energy. "He'll drink all this honey between here and Benton," Reese said, holding up a small jar three-quarters full. "He'll find a big shade tree—deep, dark shade—and I'll stop the car, and he'll drink milk and honey and read his Bible for a few minutes, then he'll brush his teeth."

A master of the stump, Johnson was perhaps even more adept at name-calling than Faubus. In just one television speech in mid-September, 1966, he branded Rockefeller the aforementioned "prissy sissy" and "Clever Manipulator," as well as a "Santa Gertrudis Steer," a "Madison Avenue Cowboy," and "the Anointed One."[9] Johnson had charisma, though he was sometimes a little wild with it. His evangelistic fervor had carried him from the state senate to the Arkansas Supreme Court on the 1958 tide of segregationist sentiment. But that sentiment had waned.

Johnson had taken a short vacation in mid-August of 1966, and his first pronouncement upon his return was that he wouldn't need the support of the Faubus administration to win. Faubus and Johnson didn't appear together at the Democratic convention. Representative Wilbur D. Mills—the only member of the state's congressional delegation to associate with Johnson publicly—made an impassioned plea designed to moderate Johnson's image as a dangerous radical.[10] David Pryor, who would win that year the state's fourth congressional district seat and later go on to the governorship, keynoted the convention with a call for party unity. But party unity wasn't there, because too many Democrats couldn't stomach Jim Johnson.

"This is the craziest campaign I've ever seen," Faubus once remarked. It became even crazier when Johnson decided he needed Faubus after all and made an effort to reconcile himself to the old pro. As the Johnson-Faubus relationship began to warm up, Rockefeller started the attack he had been saving, with the added spice of being able to say that Johnson had "betrayed the trust of his own people." One newspaper advertisement stated: "Last minute program change—Jimmy Johnson and Orval Faubus, originally scheduled to appear in "Duel Under the Oaks" will now be seen in "The Honeymooners.""

To Johnson's stream of name-calling, Rockefeller was mostly unresponsive. He had learned that he didn't help matters when he called a few names himself. But once, with only a little more than a week to go, he just couldn't stand it. In a news conference Rockefeller was asked about Johnson taking personal credit for defeat of a civil rights proposal in the Congress. Rockefeller was tired by this time, and he responded, "If you force me into giving you one answer, as I've always said, he's a conceited ass."[11] Rockefeller could be forgiven for finally not holding his tongue.

On one occasion during the "crazy" campaign, Rockefeller received a telephone call advising him that facts and figures—apparently from WR's income tax returns—were included in a pro-Johnson ad in a Jonesboro newspaper. He was stunned, since the figures were basically correct. They revealed that several of Rockefeller's enterprises were losing money, including Winrock Farms. The point of the ad, of course, was that if the man couldn't manage his own money, how could he manage the state? Sure enough, a quick check showed that some of Rockefeller's personal tax records had been taken from a file at Peat, Marwick, Mitchell and Co., an accounting firm with an office in Little Rock. Rockefeller was furious. He got on the phone and lambasted the officials of the accounting firm, the outcome of which was a white-faced conference with those officials and a higher-up executive who flew in to deal with the crisis. Rockefeller found it incredible that while he was out campaigning, dealing with the thousand and one knotty problems that plagued his campaign, something as supposedly sacrosanct as his personal tax files were being stolen and used against him. Later, a former employee of the firm was suspected of removing the Rockefeller records, but no one was ever arrested.

It didn't matter. Rockefeller had the black vote solid, and for the first time a man with the state's conservative backing would lose the election. Politicos who were analyzing the Johnson-Rockefeller confrontation said that Johnson's name-calling was a serious error. Johnson already had the hard-nosed states' righters. What he needed was some of the middle-of-the-road people, some of the very honest, sincere people out there who wanted only to vote for the man they thought would make the best governor of Arkansas. Many of them wanted to vote the Democratic ticket, if they had just had a reason for doing so. Johnson made the mistake of not giving them a reason, and Rockefeller got enough votes to win. Rockefeller ended his second race for governor with a television speech in which he said Arkansas would reject "the smears and villifications of a badly beaten man." Earlier that day, Faubus had gotten word to state employees that Johnson couldn't win. That, Johnson said later, cost him the election.

Maybe.

What did Rockefeller think? Here is how he analyzed it some years later:

> In '66 the people were not necessarily voting for me. Certainly they weren't voting for a Republican. They were voting against a system they had wearied of. They knew I was not in it for personal gain, and they were fully aware of what had transpired under my leadership in industrial development. This meant dollars in their pockets. There were many who emerged businesswise, professionally and commercially. Without the impetus, without the stimulation of the economy, they would never have gotten off dead center and might very easily have moved out of the state for greater opportunity. They saw hope for the future here. So I have the feeling that the original election [against Johnson] wasn't quite as surprising when you realize that I was running against the type of person I was.[12]

Rockefeller had given Faubus a good run for his money

in 1964, but in 1966 he really went all out, even to the extent of getting folksy on occasion when that seemed to be the ticket. He did seem more down to earth than he had been in 1964, perhaps because the people had now seen him more than once and he was a more familiar sight. Once, when he was campaigning in south Arkansas, the bus on which he was moving about the state broke down. Rockefeller and his aides flagged down a pickup truck, and WR climbed into the cab and rode to Texarkana with the farmer. The public-relations staff loved it more than WR. He made it to his speech just about on time, too, and they loved that even more.

Arriving on time was very difficult for Rockefeller. His staff simply couldn't understand how a man so thoughtful and polite in others ways could seem so indifferent to meeting deadlines. Once, an aide in charge of scheduling fund-raising get-togethers for Rockefeller tried to fool him. The aide—desperate after so many situations where Rockefeller was anywhere from thirty minutes to more than an hour late—told the candidate that an event was to begin at 7 P.M. Ironically, Rockefeller had resolved on his own that he would do better this time. Once the campaign was airborne, en route to the "7 o'clock event," the aide knew he was in trouble; but he didn't know what to say. There was no ride for them at the airport. That seemed strange, but they located transportation and got on to the house at which the reception was to be held. No one was there except the host. The campaigners stood around for a minute or two; then Rockefeller politely inquired about the guests. "They're not due until 7:30," the host replied in surprise. Rockefeller said nothing to the embarrassed aide. But he never seemed to try quite so hard to be on time after that.

For the most part, WR kept his sense of humor throughout the campaign. It was all that saved him on occasion, he sometimes said. Jerol Garrison, a reporter for the *Arkansas Gazette*, had provoked WR's good-natured ire with several accounts of the rallies at which he estimated crowds at considerably fewer than Rockefeller thought he could see out there. Rockefeller was invited to tour a twenty-story bank building under construction. The news media, including Garrison, went along. As they all stood on the sidewalk looking up at the structure already erected to its full height, Rockefeller turned to Garrison and said: "I suppose you'd estimate that as an eight-story building?"

Victory was sweet for Rockefeller, but it was slow in coming. Even on election night—when winners traditionally wave and smile before the television lights and strobe flashes of photographers—WR would be denied for a time. "The trend looks as though it is moving in my favor," Rockefeller said with caution in an appearance at his campaign headquarters, a remodeled cafeteria in downtown Little Rock. But as the evening wore on, the returns still would not yield to a declaration of clearcut victory.[13] Adding to WR's caution was the seeming fate of his running mate, Maurice "Footsie" Britt. It appeared that Britt would be defeated by James Pilkington.

David Rockefeller had flown down from New York to be with his brother on this historic night, but he avoided the spotlight as attention focused on WR. Mrs. Rockefeller was beside the governor-to-be's side, clad in a bright red dress. Other family members and friends crowded around a makeshift podium to confront a room filled with newsmen who were confident WR was to be the next governor of Arkansas. "My opponent has not conceded defeat," WR warned. "On the morrow, when he does, I will have further things to say."

Johnson conceded the next afternoon in a phoned-in statement to Democratic party headquarters.[14] By then, late returns had given Britt the lieutenant governorship. Only then did Rockefeller accept fully his victory and turn his thoughts to serving as the first Republican governor of Arkansas in ninety-four years.

CHAPTER IV

An Agonizing Adjustment

He called it a "momentous day" in his life—his inauguration as governor; and he added that it was possibly a "momentous day" in the history of Arkansas. Rockefeller expressed his hopes and fears with what was termed "unusual eloquence," calling for a "far-reaching quest for quality" and an "era of excellence." He would hear the latter term thrown back at him many times—with distortion and derision—"Aura of Arrogance," "Error of Excellence."

The four years would turn upside down a state accustomed to rubber-stamp noncontroversy in the capital. WR would turn the white heat on every problem he uncovered, more than once burning himself and many of those close to him in the process. There were no secrets in the Rockefeller administration. Many believed fervently that he would have been well advised to keep a few.

In early 1967, the euphoria of winning was still in the glassy eyes of the Rockefeller organization. An opinion poll was run to track just how popular he was and what sort of public support could be expected to make itself felt on the legislators who would try to fight Rockefeller without ruining themselves with constituents who just might want the man to have some help in the capital. The poll delivered by Gene Newsom on January 23 added to the euphoria.[1] "We get Mr. Rockefeller at an extremely high 80 percent on the favorability side of the attitude scale. Jim Johnson has all but disappeared from the scene."

Things were looking up, but there was an ominous sign passing almost unnoticed that would later manifest itself darkly. The threat was in a segment in the pollster's summary that began with this query: "The Republicans have a chance now to make good on their promises and I want to see Rockefeller put his program through. Agree or disagree?" The electorate was nine-to-one agreeable. "However," the pollster warned, "we get slightly above a third of the voters saying that they would like to see the legislature hold Rockefeller back on some of the ideas he has." Later, legislators would find in this public attitude a sort of "license" to "hold Rockefeller back" by trying to destroy his programs.

The new governor began his administration by irritating the legislators. He chose to make his inaugural speech in Robinson Auditorium, which would seat three thousand, instead of in the house chamber, which would seat the legislators and a few friends in the galleries. He did agree to speak briefly in the chamber, on his way to the auditorium for his principal remarks; but the lawmakers wouldn't be mollified. Many of them didn't even bother to trail him down to Robinson Auditorium. "We come here committed not to discord, but to doing," he said in the auditorium speech; but the seeds were already sown for more discord than had ever been witnessed by a staid citizenry or an excited and appreciative press.[2]

"I am well aware," Rockefeller continued, "of the pride represented in this Sixty-sixth General Assembly. It is true that you and I have been allotted an unusual moment in Arkansas history, a moment subject to special scrutiny—laden with special challenges and rich with special opportunities."

Meanwhile, members of the senate were completing their plans to jam through more than ninety appointments made by Orval Faubus, without offering the new governor the customary privilege of reviewing them. Some politicos claimed that Rockefeller had set himself up for such treatment by circulating an unsigned, mimeographed note to legislators, requesting the chance to review the appointments before the senate confirmed them. They knew that Faubus would never have made that mistake, would have contacted them in person. Rockefeller, they said, would have to learn to be as accessible as Faubus was. But the new governor knew that his mimeographed plea wasn't the reason for the senate action. As a matter of fact, his aides had heard of the plan to rush the appointments through, and the note was mimeographed because that was the quickest way to reach all in an attempt to head off the action.

In fact, Rockefeller observed, "some of them said they ignored my note because it wasn't signed. But we told them, 'Aw, come on' and they admitted they probably would have anyway. I wrote them a conciliatory letter, and I've been talking to them in the past couple of days, and I think we're getting it ironed out." But it wouldn't really be "ironed out" until Rockefeller left office.

When people from the towns and boondocks of Arkansas got to the legislature they had a sense of self-importance; they were swelled up a bit. Each felt like he had bested opposition that Rockefeller was either directly or indirectly responsible for. The fact that he got anything at all done under such circumstances is amazing.

Republicans, a number of them anyway, felt that WR forsook the party after he won, that he left the party too much alone and devoted himself solely to the problems of government. Leaving the party structure unattended—in the hands of the people who were willing to work day in and day out even in the nonpolitical season—WR allowed the party to be taken over by others. Rockefeller didn't intervene, and anti-Rockefeller Republicans saw their opportunity. But the crux of the matter was really patronage, a subject on which the governor's philosophy was at odds with the traditional Arkansas approach. About patronage, WR said: "I was very much aware of the fact that for reelection I was still going to be dependent on the independent and Democratic vote. So with those people who had worked for me as Independents or Citizens for Rockefeller that were known Democrats, I made appointments from those ranks—first, if I felt that there were individuals that were more competent, and second, deliberately, in the use of that power of patronage to maintain the kind of a relationship that I needed with the Democratic majority."[3]

Some of his closest aides believed that good government was good politics. But there was a strong patronage group that simply said, "Fire every state employee, fill every job with a Republican or supporter." They'll still argue that one of his greatest mistakes was that he didn't do so. But nobody was under any misconception about what the new governor was going to do. He would try to find the best man for every job, and he would not fire state employees without good cause.

Rockefeller selected people he felt were qualified, gave them his ideas about the goals of the job, discussed with them conditionally the means of implementing those goals, and then turned them loose. "There was a feeling of organizational responsibility, organizational latitude, and personal involvement which brought out the best in the people working for me," he once said. "If you have that kind of an administration and an organization, then you are freer to do the broader scale things. We were tremendously aware," he continued, "that my predecessor was the manager of a one-man government. And he had lieutenants. During the course of my administration, the governor was the captain of a team of administrators who were given the maximum of latitude and responsibility. And they were allowed to function within the legal definition of their job without constant interference from the governor's office."[4]

The internal fight over the matter of party-building represented a kind of philosophical split from the very beginning among Republicans; it presented the kind of dilemma that Rockefeller faced all through his political career. Was everything fine until he got into office and then threw the party aside? No. Not really. Philosophical differences between the Republican party and Rockefeller were there from the start.

Soon after his election and before he took office, Rockefeller invited Education Commissioner A. W. "Arch" Ford and Welfare Commissioner A. J. "Red" Moss to continue in their present jobs. This angered even a few of those closest to Rockefeller. The governor was offering logic when the Republicans wanted patronage. About Moss, he said, "I don't think anyone in the state or maybe the nation knows forwards and backwards the welfare regulations like he does." Rockefeller said it would be a serious mistake for the Republican party to "run everybody off for partisan politics." He added that in the normal course over the next two years there would be "plenty of opportunities for us to reward dedicated followers." Rockefeller said Republicans would have first claim for openings and the Democrats for Rockefeller second; but in either case, he maintained, the jobs would go to competent persons.[5] To those who equated competence with Republicanism, his words were not warmly received.

Faubus characterized Rockefeller's problems with patronage by saying, "It's a part of politics. It always has been, although it's a burden." Faubus noted that you cannot handle patronage in such a way as to reelect yourself, but you can handle it in such a way as to get defeated. He described the situation as nearly all debit and very little credit:

> Alright, to whom is Rockefeller going to listen? To the people who brought in the votes for him, who contributed? The legislators, the majority of them, have always had a hand in this and when they get down there, they're imbued with their importance. I could work with them and dovetail it with my organi-

zation for the most part. Rockefeller could not. When he listened to the legislature, for the most part, he was going against those people out there who had really elected him.

But you had a legislature overwhelmingly dominated by Democrats. Whereas, out in the counties, many of them, Rockefeller had gotten a majority of the votes and according to all the rules of the game, he was supposed to listen to them.[6]

Rockefeller did his best to break down that natural partisan barrier to progress; but so often, he came off sounding either "holier than thou" or scolding. In the inaugural address, he had said, "Now is the time to put politics behind us. I was elected by Republicans, Democrats and Independents. I intend to represent all." The Democrats didn't like that, and a lot of Republicans—who had never had anything except some post office jobs when a Republican president took office—didn't like it either. WR kept trying to find qualified Republicans, it's true. But in the meantime, he appointed many Democrats, and the howls may still echo at times in Republican county committee meetings.

"I believe that together we can become worthy of this moment," Rockefeller said in his inaugural. "We shall make mistakes. That is to be expected. But we shall also right ourselves, because we share the same goals." He was wrong on that last point. The legislators, most of them anyway, didn't share his goals.

Just four weeks into the first legislative session, his frustration already mounting, Rockefeller said: "A few men have attempted to choke off the development of better government in Arkansas . . . to embarrass the new state administration in every way possible. . . . They have attempted to show, at any cost, that a Republican governor cannot possibly accomplish anything with a legislature made up almost entirely of Democrats. I have never believed this and I do not believe it now. I am confident that most of you do not either. I must tell you now—in the most emphatic terms—that I will not sit quietly in the governor's office while a few legislators do their best to dismantle the executive branch of government. I was not elected for that and neither were you."[7] But the legislators hardly noticed, as they set about, many of them, to strip him of all the power they could and set up their own controls.

Rockefeller was naively hopeful from the beginning of his official involvement in things political that the ideas he held for Arkansas would be implemented because he would win the support of legislators who could and would work with him on programs that were good for Arkansas. On various occasions after he filed in 1964, he was questioned closely by the media. Should he win, he would face a legislature largely made up of Democrats. How would he fare with them? WR knew many of the legislators, and truly believed that enough were conscientious and sincere, wanting only what was best for their constituents, that they would help him with his programs. Those programs, he would explain with earnest if faulty logic, were designed for the people of Arkansas, and because of that the lawmakers no doubt would support them.

At first he was bewildered by the partisanship, but it didn't take him long to see that the rules in the legislature and the principles he had been reared on were in almost total conflict. He soon realized that a legislator could break bread with him in the morning, expressing virtual agreement with him and his goals, but before noon of that same day the same legislator could attack administration programs with merciless personal ridicule and derision.

But good government versus good politics—in terms of patronage—was not the only area of conflict for the new governor. There were other adjustments, other more personal issues that created almost immediate unrest.

Although Rockefeller took office in January, he did not take up residence in the governor's mansion until October. He and Mrs. Rockefeller moved into a penthouse apartment across the street from the state capitol, a move that reinforced the doubts of some about whether he thought the mansion—or the office of governor, for that matter— was good enough for him. Although he explained more than once that the delay was to allow time for renovation, some hinted openly that the tradition against liquor being served in the mansion was an important reason for his long wait before moving there. It wasn't. If he wanted a drink, Rockefeller had one, with no attempt at secrecy. In fact, on more than one controversial occasion, Rockefeller was as cheerfully candid about having a drink in the morning be- fore a tough day at the capitol as he was about everything else.

When vexed, he could be quite blunt. Rockefeller hated to hear an unanswered phone ringing; and many a routine business caller to Winrock gulped in surprise when the owner answered. The same situation prevailed at the man- sion. During the difficulties over patronage (when legis- lators wanted to continue "handling" state jobs in their counties and districts while Rockefeller was trying to ac- commodate the Republican party without retreating from his principles by putting an unqualified partisan in a job he couldn't handle), the party chairman complained that Rockefeller was inaccessible. WR replied that every drunk in Arkansas seemed to be able to get him on the phone at all hours of the night and that surely the party chairman could be equally enterprising.

The whole mansion controversy annoyed Rockefeller; he thought about it a good deal. "The very nature of life at the Mansion was restricting," Rockefeller recalled later; "and therefore, where my normal pattern of life would have in- volved using the mansion more and cultivating small groups of people who could exert influence, I did not find the Mansion life conducive to that end, and therefore did not follow it."[8] He did find the prevailing attitudes about serving liquor there uncomfortable. "I admitted that I'd had a drink. The vast majority of people who are used to having a cocktail or a drink before dinner and/or wine or drinks after dinner, find an evening that is artificial not terribly rewarding. The fact that you could not be normal and act as you would in your own home or the home of your friends was stifling."[9]

Rockefeller said that visitors could come to the mansion at any time of the day or night while he occupied it and find him behaving in a manner consistent with the public position he had taken in favor of the mixed drink bill. "What I did in my home was consistent with what I do in my home today and what I did in my home before," Rockefeller said, explaining that the upstairs of the mansion was his home and the downstairs was the public building. With some adaptation of our style of living, WR added, "we accepted for ourselves essentially apartment-type living and did not entertain as much as I would have liked because of the tradition of the Mansion as it stood in the minds of so many people. We never served any alcoholic beverages in the public part of the building, not even wine."[10]

Part of the reason that Rockefeller was charged with being inaccessible was that he insisted on maintaining work habits that were considerably different from those of his predecessor. As his speech writer Charles Allbright once commented, "He didn't attend many terrapin derbies." Nor did he issue inane proclamations or wield big scissors at ribbon-cuttings, even though most politicians in Arkansas traditionally worked such occasions to the fullest for political "mileage." Rockefeller felt they were a waste of time, and someone else on the staff fell heir to them. Even so Rockefeller wasn't necessarily at the capitol office while his subordinates filled in for him. In fact, he was hardly ever there. He made little apology for his un-availability, despite continual carping by the press and others. He said that the governor's office was geared for ceremonial functions, and in order to get anything creative and worthwhile done, he had to think about it. He could do that better, he argued, in the privacy of the governor's mansion or at Winrock. Some believed him. Others didn't. But through it all, even in the campaigns, he refused to bend very much. And the campaign years saw the organization insisting, if futilely, that "the governor's office is where he is."

He was a man really apart from everyone else, because he appeared incapable of maintaing a normal one-to-one relationship with anyone. He would not reveal himself. As a matter of fact, every person who knew him would offer an entirely different view of the man. No one ever saw the whole man. He would show one person this part and another that; but he never really let anyone see him fully as he was. He was a man apart in that sense, and people tended to keep him apart. He tried in 1964 particularly to be folksy. But most people who knew him didn't want him to be one of the guys. And he really never was. Jeannette Rockefeller once said, "Win is a little bit like the tip of an iceberg. . . . There's so much underneath in terms of what Win is and how he thinks that never comes to the surface that people think of him as being one kind of a person or another kind when in reality he's many people."

Rockefeller brought an entirely different set of values to the political scene in Arkansas. To him, the governor's office was a means to an end, the route through which he could accomplish certain things. To others, the office had been an end to itself, a place they were going to. When they had gained that place, they had everything. But to Rockefeller, life as governor wasn't the end of the rainbow; indeed, this was a step down for him, in terms of his standard of living. He had his own style about everything, and he refused to fit the mold created by the habits of his predecessors. Arkansas' new governor even complained openly about the poor taste and ratty condition of his office. Political friends were horrified at his comments. But he stuck to his guns, once observing with sardonic amusement that the office's snack bar—where his proverbial peanut butter and crackers were stored—was in the toilet. His successor got the appropriation to remodel the offices.

Another "different" feature of this governor (and one often criticized) was the fact that an entourage of aides was seen with him practically everywhere. The women, if efficient, were also pretty; and the men were mostly youngish and ambitious. A bodyguard was always in evidence (there had been threats on Rockefeller's life), and a frequent complaint was that one couldn't get to Rockefeller for the phalanx of aides and bodyguards that just seemed to grow up around him. On occasion, he would reluctantly put aside his good-natured generosity and run most of them off. Once, when a self-appointed aide was clutching WR's elbow to move him toward another prospective voter, Rockefeller—who never liked to stop anything he was enjoying—jerked his arm away in irritation and instructed the aide to "go take a tranquilizer." But for the most part he tolerated the group well, even enjoyed them when the end-of-day relaxing began. And perhaps they enjoyed his company even more than he enjoyed theirs. The jealousy that prevailed among the aides and between the different offices that Rockefeller maintained suggested a possessiveness on the part of the governor's staff members. Offices competed constantly for Rockefeller to call this one or that one "home" and spend his time there.

His business office, 1720 Tower Building, was plush and cold. He stayed there for the election returns in all his races. Thereafter his visits to this office were duty ones, when an important business matter absolutely required his presence or personal signature, or when morale had degenerated to the point that he had to drop by and cheer everyone up with a "Hello." Ten floors down, at 790 Tower Building, was his personal office, occupied by his former secretary at Winrock, Jane Bartlett. She moved with him when he won the governorship. The governor set her up in this two-room suite to handle his personal correspondence. Among the offices stocked with politically oriented late-comers, she found that it wasn't always easy to get hold of the mail. Two or three individuals in each of the other offices wanted all the personal material they could possibly divert to their desks, to use for getting closer to the man some of them called "Big Daddy Two Boots."

In Suite 530 of the same building was the party-oriented office. Here were those on the payroll, mainly holdovers from his party-building days. Some of the inhabitants of that office met him elsewhere. There was less hassling that way. Everett Ham, a top aide in that office, insecure and nervous by now at what he viewed as Rockefeller's virtual abandonment of concern about the GOP, would always greet WR at the door when he stopped by, guide him into his office, close the door, and launch into long private talks while everyone else Rockefeller wanted to see waited outside wondering what was going on. Not much was, as it turned out. Rockefeller found himself mostly listening. He finally stopped going there altogether.

Then there was Suite 222, in a building nearer the capitol; this housed the public-relations staff, which had moved from the 530 suite at Rockefeller's request. The governor spent much of his time at 222, setting up meetings there with state officials and others. It was a plush office, to say the least. The decor was the nicest of any of WR's Little Rock offices, in the opinion of many; and it earned the envy of those in the other offices, who frequently had to call Rockefeller there if they wanted to talk to him at all.

The PR office, as it came to be known, was a place where WR could "put his feet up," as he said. It had a kitchen and a bar, and Rockefeller had a favorite chair there. PR wound up with the reputation of "running the state," but the charge was not accurate. What happened was that WR would invite principals for important, decision-making meetings to meet him there, and much vital policy was made in the physical surroundings of PR. But the PR folks were not involved in many of those decisions.

One newspaper publisher, Perrin Jones of Searcy, commented on Rockefeller's threatening to fire his entire public-relations staff for failing to keep him informed sufficiently so that he could make speeches. Jones said that previous Arkansas governors, without WR's resources, had had to make speeches and prepare themselves for public appearances by the simple expedient of learning something about the subject. According to Jones, WR had one of the finest public-relations staffs ever put together and his ability to stay in office was due in no small measure to that staff and its polished handling of "a most inept administration."[11]

Rockefeller had a reasonable amount of confidence in the public-relations office, but he didn't think the folks there were the greatest thing since baling wire. Indeed, he was most aware that this staff—a sizable collection of people dedicated to presenting the best possible image of Rockefeller while assisting him in the affairs of state—often found itself the focal point of the news instead of the manager of it. This fact often made Rockefeller either lose his temper about this office, or loyally defend its plushness and its personnel. On occasion he felt obliged to remark, with some resentment, that his public-relations office didn't necessarily run him, that as a matter of fact it would be kind of hard to "run" Win Rockefeller. He was, he would continue, grateful for the advice of those in the office with whom he consulted.

But WR had had a lifetime of experience at being set upon with all sorts of guidance and advice, as well as with schemes to help him spend his money, and it was a rare person or group that could really influence him. In fact,

much of the course of his life—the service aspect of
it—was set very early, and there is no question but that the
profoundest influence of all came from his parents, particularly his mother. He agreed with a New York newspaper's comment that "their grandfather and father made
them millionaires, but their mother made them men."
Rockefeller said his mother taught him and his brothers
human feeling. "She was no more impressed by some
great dignitary than by some simple working man."[12]

With all he learned from his family and others, however,
WR was always essentially a private person, one who
found it difficult to open the doors and allow the press and
everyone else to tramp through. Bob Faulkner, WR's administrative assistant for the last two of his years in the
governor's office, said Rockefeller knew or sensed that he
was not able to stand the kind of exposure the office required. "The private man was rebelling even then. He
never was able to let himself sit there in that white light
eight hours a day in the governor's office and let the public
come, look and see and poke and question and so on. He
always lived a life ostensibly as a public man but never as a
public man."[13]

That private man dreaded asking favors of people. It was
as if he were afraid he'd be asked one in return; or perhaps
he simply disliked invading the privacy of another. At any
rate, the staff routinely provided Rockefeller with lists of
people to call in various towns and cities he visited, with
the idea of recruiting them into the campaign effort or lin-
ing up a campaign contribution. Just as routinely, Rockefeller never got around to calling any of them.

Why did WR get involved in politics? Was he seeking
some goal that would give him light, happiness, peace?
He'd tried just about everything. He'd searched everywhere—in his family, at school, in the oil fields, and in the
infantry. Although he never really found what he was
seeking, he came closer to it in the service than anywhere

else. But one doesn't make a career of the military if one's name is Rockefeller, someone once remarked about WR. He didn't find what he was looking for in New York's cafe society; he didn't find it in cattle ranching; and he didn't find it in politics, either.

According to Eisele, Rockefeller had a strong sense of family—and a strong feeling that he was the maverick of his own family, the one who might not be measuring up.

> He continually assaulted himself with the attitude of his contribution as a Rockefeller to the tradition. And of course, this thinking in Arkansas was great. It must have given him satisfaction and independence. He had lived in the shadow of his great brothers. He'd been kind of put down by the others. He'd been the little brother, although not the youngest. Still he was the one that they all kind of kept an eye out for. But in a way, he was more independent than they. And he certainly took on challenges that you have to say none of them did. They went right into the traditional things—banking or politics, if you want to put it that way. For a Rockefeller to come to the South and to make it down here, I don't know if it gave him that sense of achievement, but it was a fantastic success story. Still, he wanted to be accepted by the family, he still wanted their approval, and yet there were two things, a reaction against them as well as wanting it. You almost have the feeling that he intentionally did things on occasion that destroyed that possibility.[14]

In some ways—with his zeal for changing things—Rockefeller was like a nineteenth-century missionary. Yet, he was totally different in that he was constantly searching for a better way himself. He wanted others to be like him, if only in terms of fighting against conformity or keeping their minds open to new ideas. He had an insatiable desire for new ideas, and he could pick out a workable one from all he heard with a fair amount of consistency. But in almost every case he consistently stayed so far ahead that few could visualize with him what he saw for himself and others. Mrs. Rockefeller later said, "I finally realized that it was almost impossible for many people to accept the fact that here was a man doing this because of his beliefs and not because he wanted anything except to see that others had a better life than before. It was so foreign to anything that many people had known about a public person. They couldn't believe there wasn't something underneath that he wanted. They knew it wasn't money."[15]

Yet, despite all this determination to be the catalyst for change, Rockefeller was often more fearful than he indicated, particularly in large crowds. For example, the April 16, 1969, memorial service for Martin Luther King, Jr., on the steps of the state capitol precipitated many hours of reflection afterward. With three thousand persons assembled on the capitol steps, Rockefeller said, he was fearful because he was surrounded by buildings where anyone with a rifle "could have done personal damage and harm." Rockefeller felt conspicuous, aware of the possibility of a fanatic with a high-powered rifle.

But all his fear about such people notwithstanding, Rockefeller basically liked to imagine that he saw growth and development in those around him. And indeed, he could be a real stimulus for such changes. That memorial service gave him his first good look at a militant black minister named Cecil Cone. Cone offered some fiery oratory, and Rockefeller sensed that the minister's words were having a very disturbing effect on the already-tense crowd. Rockefeller pulled on Cone's arm, stopped his talk, and the two men became closer afterward.

About Cone and other black leaders, Rockefeller said that they were thorns in his side; but because he always stood his ground, he believed he gained their respect and got an opportunity to develop his own respect for them. And that, he said, "strengthened the usefulness of us both. No question but that if both of us had not had the self-confidence to accept the other, and the logic and reasoning of the other, that would never have happened."

Rockefeller actually tried to win Cone over. And he felt

that he was at least partly successful. His early training, he said, helped in this sort of thing. Early in life, he learned that you don't just accept life as it comes down the road; you have a part in it. "There were many aspects to our upbringing which focused attention on that basic philosophy that 'You reap what you sow,'" he said. And attending a progressive school nurtured this tendency to take positions and try things without feelings of restraint. "You learned by your mistakes but not with the guilt complex that so many children develop in the more pedestrian-type schools," he said.[16]

Rockefeller was far more interested in helping people help themselves than he was in giving them outright financial gifts, though he did a lot of the latter. He explained that philosophy this way:

> Experience will tell you very quickly that the person whom you help to help himself profits and benefits far more than any monetary assistance that you could give him in total. And similarly, if you get involved in a project that's got to have continuity and leadership on down through the years ahead, one capable of making private contributions as I am is pouring money down the drain if you don't build supportive interest through financial participation or physical participation in whatever the project may be. You can be a great hero for today by making a financial contribution out of proportion—be the only one—but being a practical person, I just cannot sit by and watch a substantial sum of money be spent and no results to show for it. So this is a reflection of a philosophy of getting personal involvement on the part of other people to pick up the load of many projects I have been interested in and have not infrequently spawned, if you will. But they would have died of their own weight without competent leadership and continuity.[17]

That streak of practicality in philanthropic matters manifested itself in WR's private life as well. Rockefeller called his friend Jack Pickens one morning and told him he had to go to Korea that very afternoon to represent the president of the United States. He talked for a good long while, told Pickens about the trip, and commented, "You know what tickles me, Pickens? My cutaway and my striped trousers fit me perfectly. I've lost 17 pounds. I don't have to have one thing done to them. I got them out and tried them on." Finally, Pickens recalled, Rockefeller said, "What I really called you about . . . do you have a pair of gray gloves and a gray ascot tie that I could wear with my cutaway and striped trousers?" Pickens (who had begun his highly successful business career as a laborer in a brickyard) answered, "Goddamn, Rockefeller, are you calling down here to ask a dropout from a brickyard something like that? Hell, I've never had a cutaway or a pair of striped britches in my life, let alone a gray ascot and a pair of gloves. Why don't you borrow your son's that he used over at Williamsburg last month?" Plaintively Rockefeller confided, "He rented them. I guess that's what I'll have to do."[18]

Rockefeller's frugality was the subject of many a reporter's half-serious, half-cynical observations; but the reporters got bluntly serious when they discussed the governor's frugality with his time in terms of gubernatorial responsibilities. One radio station began to make hourly reports on how many hours it had been since the governor had been in his office at the capitol. This irritated Rockefeller no end. He said that the habits of his predecessor were never thus publicized. The press's inordinate concern with his every move caused Rockefeller to say: "I think that the press, because I was such a contrast [to Faubus],brought into focus the idea of a daily bulletin."[19]

It is true that the media took a great deal more account of Rockefeller, at least in part simply because he was a Rockefeller. They had never been that close to one. Rockefeller noted their confusion between the governor and the man, saying they "interwove them without the maturity to see that they were doing it." In a sophisticated environment such as New York, he explained, "the governor's personal life is basically not newsworthy."[20]

WR showed up at the capitol one day about 3:30 P.M., posed for a couple of pictures, held a brief news conference, and headed elsewhere. George Douthit, a newsman, called out, "Sure was a short day" and drove away before WR could answer. That night about 10:30, Douthit was awakened by a phone call. The voice said, "This is Governor Rockefeller. I just wanted you to know that I am still working."

Party patronage and personal habits were only two, though two very large, issues on which Rockefeller's philosophy was from the outset at odds with Arkansas politics. But these philosophical differences would lie at the root of almost every particular problem the new governor would confront.

CHAPTER V

WR as Governor

Some legislators viewed the new Republican governor with great caution. Senator Lee Bearden of Leachville, second ranking in point of seniority, said, "Those who oppose Rockefeller's programs just on the basis of political party are making a sad mistake." Some listened to Bearden, but not many.

One of his friends said Rockefeller got into politics because he thought he could do something for Arkansas, "and Lord knows, he tried. But with a Democratic legislature, he didn't have the chance of a snowball in hell." Yet, he accomplished a good deal in spite of the Democratic lawmakers, at least in part because the legislators didn't dislike Rockefeller for his differences and his Republicanism as much as they might have resented some "traitor" to their system—a local product, in other words. After all, this man was a New Yorker, rich, a Republican, and a Rockefeller. He was supposed to be different.

In his speech to the joint session after the first general assembly of his administration had been underway a few weeks, Rockefeller said that general revenues had increased by about 20 percent, but he warned that the dramatic jump was because of a double tax collection, owing to passage of the income tax withholding law. This was true, but Rockefeller had a difficult time convincing anybody. The windfall, he explained, would not reoccur. He outlined his fiscal policy to the lawmakers and urged them not to take actions that would undermine the programs and policies of the state, not only for that present biennium but for the next one as well.

Rockefeller recommended increased allotments for the universities and colleges, a $5-per-month increase for welfare recipients, a $500-a-year raise for teachers, and modest salary increases for employees of the cities and counties. The governor acknowledged that his requests were modest, but he reminded the legislators that "the only available alternative to the approach which I have suggested is an increase in taxes."[1]

He had their attention.

Rockefeller urged that the lawmakers enable the state to use more of the balances in various state accounts, because with income tax collections such balances weren't required. The necessary legislation was provided. Rockefeller also asked for some other things, the most notable of which was the creation of a state administration department for coordinating a number of state functions. The legislators gave him that too. But even in that session, they became progressively less cooperative. And Rockefeller was learning fast that the governor's office wasn't all-powerful. In fact, he was most surprised at the limited powers available to him. He said that the legislators, acting in fear, worked increasingly to limit his power. Rockefeller laid the blame in part on his being a Republican. "It is an admission of defeat if you can't by persuasion appeal to most people," he said later. "I don't mind fighting a man on whatever level he wants to fight, as long as there is a basis for his rationale. But when it's just purely and simply disruptive, divisive and sabotaging for partisan politics, I think that's about as frustrating a problem as any governor would face."[2]

But none of this was so evident as Rockefeller plunged into his first session with the legislature, full of enthusiasm and undaunted by charges that he and his staff were unprepared. The truth is, more could perhaps have been done in terms of mechanics, but a great deal of preparation had been made in the short time between the general election and WR's taking office. It could nevertheless be said fairly that the fledgling governor and his aides had tried to cover so much ground, to deal with so many needs they had been studying for the past three or four years that their efforts were spread too thin. The result was a lot of proposals, but a not very clear picture of the governor's program. At any rate, what was accomplished in that first session—January 9–March 10 and March 27–31—was nothing short of amazing.

Among the administration measures that became acts were those providing free high school textbooks, establishing drivers' education in the public schools, creating a constitutional study commission, providing for the issuance of drivers' licenses on a staggered basis, prohibiting the issuance of drivers' licenses to persons legally classified as blind, providing for motor vehicle inspection as a prerequisite for licensing, establishment of prison industries, creation of a governmental efficiency study commission, and creation of the aforementioned state administration department and a personnel division for it. Also enacted were several measures for tightening up insurance regulations and a measure to provide an increase in welfare grants. Rockefeller lost some, too. Bills to provide tenure for public school teachers and to restrict political activities of state employees were defeated; street and highway classification didn't pass, nor did the minimum wage proposal. Efforts to create an agriculture development commission and a "wheel" system for selecting jurors also failed.

When it was over, some political observers felt that Arkansas had stumbled its way into the era of two-party politics; but nobody was saying that the state, the legislature, or the governor was at peace about it all. Rockefeller—after making some negative comments that were borne of his frustration at not getting certain things he asked of the lawmakers—decided he ought to think positively about what had happened; and when it was over he observed for the press that the legislature was "a lot better than many people have sensed or felt."

But it wasn't enough; the first special session of his administration was called on February 5, 1968, and it continued until February 21. Even though this one was more abrasive than the regular session had been, Rockefeller still felt he had gotten a good bit accomplished. Sixty-seven acts were passed, and there were some good things among them. Several measures again dealt with tighter regulations for insurance companies, and this time the governor got his minimum wage law. Another thing Rockefeller wanted badly and got from this special session was the reconstitution of the penitentiary board as the board of correction and the creation of a parole board to go with it. This was just the beginning of the new governor's efforts in the area of prison reform. Those accomplishments, as well as the trouble that accompanied them, are discussed at length in Chapter 6.

There was a lot of needless talk at the session, Rockefeller said afterward, but he termed it a productive one. His greatest disappointment was obviously the failure of the lawmakers to approve a bill to allow him to name Lynn Davis as state police director. Davis just didn't meet the existing residency requirements (ten years in Arkansas), and Davis' argument that his "heart" had always been in Arkansas didn't seem to make any difference to the legislators.

When Davis took over operations of the state police, until his qualifications (or lack of them) could be decided, he set about to clean up some flagrant illegalities that had been part of the Arkansas scene for years. He had a flair for publicity, and the media got some great pictures and great quotes as Davis personally took sledge hammer in hand and set about wrecking slot machines confiscated in Hot Springs raids. If anything, though, Davis may have talked to the media a bit too much. Rockefeller and his aides at times worried that the state's top policeman might be hurting himself and the administration with all the publicity.

On one occasion, he confided to the people about tips he had received before raiding some notable gambling spots in Little Rock and Hot Springs. A grand jury wanted to hear more about his sources of information, but Davis clammed up and was jailed for his refusal to disclose this information. The jailing of the state police director was a media dream, and Mrs. Davis made the story even better when she showed up at the Pulaski County jail with a set of clean sheets for her husband's cot. The whole affair made Davis into a folk hero, though he was released after a very short time.[3] Hero or not, however, he couldn't meet the residency requirement for a state police director and was thus moved from that post into a position on WR's payroll. He would later run for secretary of state as one of the "Five for the Future"—a group of Republicans whose candidacies for statewide office were financed by Rockefeller.

Rockefeller called the first special session "historic." He highlighted all the many things that had been accomplished, brushing aside questions and comments about the session not being needed. But disaster awaited him the next time around. He called a session for May 20, which lasted for ten days and was described by Rockefeller afterward as "fiscally irresponsible." During this session, his tax program was wrecked by the legislators. They also killed his proposal to legalize and tax mixed drinks. He threatened to recall the legislators for yet another special session. "In certain areas," the governor said, "I may suggest that some of the actions not taken were actions of irresponsibility." Rockefeller referred to some of the actions the legislators *did* take as "unbelievable stupidities."[4] One of these, according to the governor, was their approval of $500,000 for additional nursing home payments,

$200,000 more than was available in the state's rapidly depleting reserve accounts.

As far as the citizenry in general was concerned, however, the governor was still getting high marks after six months in office. They gave him credit for trying. Even when there was disagreement with him philosophically, his constituents took the view that he was in there pitching for all he was worth, and they admired him for it.

But if the governor needed any reminder that there was an abysmal apathy—or, almost as bad, ignorance—out there among the electorate, he got it when he sought the public's attitude toward a proposal he was considering for a turnpike. "There are a number," the pollster reported, "who don't even know what a turnpike is."

The governor was confused, unsure of how to respond to such information. He had followed the advice of pollsters before and it had seemed to create more problems for him than it solved. For example, after numerous entreaties from Republicans, he had appointed Dotson Collins as labor commissioner. A longtime Rockefeller ally, Collins was a hard-line Republican and a member of a Teamsters' local. Leaders of the AFL-CIO—of yellow-dog Democrat orientation—were furious about the appointment. They publicly expressed their anger over not being consulted, and their chagrin was intensified by the fact that WR had ignored the AFL-CIO executive committee's recommendations (all Democrats) for the job. These grievances, as well as the fact that these union men detested Collins, made for an awkward situation. And the governor didn't help matters any when he responded to inquiries about why he hadn't consulted the union leadership before making the appointment with "What do I owe them?".

A storm of controversy erupted over that remark, orchestrated by the AFL-CIO leaders, and Rockefeller became stubbornly silent. Later, he remembered his statement this way: "I believe I said it would not be inappropriate if organized labor had a seat on the Commission, but I never promised them one."⁵ But the "What do I owe labor" remark was what people remembered, and it was hurled back at WR in many ways. Senator J. William Fulbright labeled the remark as "stupid" among other things, then added, "Maybe I'd better withdraw the word 'stupid.'" Rockefeller wasn't so much angered as hurt by Fulbright's observation; and he responded when asked about it, "Not being a Rhodes scholar, I don't think I could have summed the remark up so succinctly in one word."

Meanwhile, union leader J. Bill Becker was saying that while the governor "certainly doesn't owe us anything, he told us that it was inconceivable that labor was not appointed to boards and commissions and he cited the Board of Education and the AIDC [Arkansas Industrial Development Commission] as examples. Certainly, it was not a promise but it was implicit in his remarks."⁶

Rockefeller stoutly defended Collins as long as the Huntsville Republican was in the position. And Collins' tenure was by no means all negative. Two months after his appointment, Collins and the governor found themselves on the capitol steps before some 2,500 persons who were concerned about an Ottenheimer garment factory strike that had dragged on for more than a year. Shouts and cheers followed Rockefeller's announcement that he had set a date for all parties to get together around the conference table. They met; and the throng that had marched in orderly fashion from Robinson Auditorium through the downtown section, singing and shouting as they went, felt something was being accomplished.

The governor's popularity had begun to decline in earnest by October, even though the opposition remained fractured as the regrouping and realignment slowly proceeded. By November the picture was even gloomier, though WR held his strength among blacks and younger voters. Despite the fact that every chief executive's popularity drops, usually some six months after inauguration, WR's staff was unsettled by the blunt reality that approval ratings of the governor had dropped about ten points and disapproval had risen correspondingly. In December, 1967, Rockefeller's popularity ratings were even lower, and this would certainly affect legislative matters unless some improvements in the governor's image were achieved.

Two factors directly related to the decline in WR's popularity were his unavailability and his lack of rapport with the electorate. If the governor could spend more time seeing people—in person, on the spot, in his office—there was reason to think his popularity with the voters might rise. Aides and friends were becoming nervous at the way things were going in terms of their man's image. As usual, they were divided over how to deal with the problems. Those closest to the governor wanted him to establish better lines to Democrats, become more accessible to them and others who wanted to see him. They also urged him to get the legislators into his office for conferences, consult them more on appointments.

Others wanted the governor to appoint more Republicans, to get out in the boondocks more to see the Republican leadership that had worked so hard to get him elected in the first place but who were being ignored. Meanwhile, the Democrats—some of whom had worked pretty hard to get Rockefeller into office so they'd have a chance to take over their own party—were looking for a good Democratic horse to ride.

And Rockefeller himself was strangely aloof from any fears about his reelection chances. One got the distinct feeling that he never entertained the idea that he might be a one-term governor; and bombarding him with the more and more gloomy poll statistics had little effect. Since he never requested or received anything like an objective weekly report of public opinion anyway, the figures had

little reality for him. He would half-listen while agitated
aides tried to describe the various things that needed to be
done. Since most of those things went against his grain—
calling people on the telephone to ask their help, kow-
towing to legislators' egos, spending more time in the
governor's office, getting up earlier and staying visible
longer—he would resolve to do better, but he never did.
Much of the advice irritated Rockefeller, who felt he had
been spending more time with the people than ever before.
But his efforts at availability seemed either inadequate or
unsuccessful.

A significant number of Arkansans had come to believe
that Rockefeller had a bad case of "foot in mouth" disease,
after he had made a few statements that were as damaging
to him as they were quotable. Naturally, the Democrats
made the most of them, right down to the cartoons showing Rockefeller with one of his boots firmly in place in his
mouth and one of these quotes beneath as the caption.

It seemed clear that Rockefeller had failed to live up to
the hopes of the voters, even though he had impressed
them with bringing in new industry, stimulating growth
and prosperity in the state. He had failed to be the type of
good governor the people had hoped for, and many no
longer believed he was aware of their problems. There was
less confidence in his ability to handle the financial affairs
of the state. Some thought that he was neglecting his job
by traveling too much; some felt he had appointed too
many out-of-state people to responsible positions, thereby
removing some highly qualified officials. There were also
complaints that an air of confusion seemed present in his
administration. A few even volunteered that he had ne-
glected older people.

Rockefeller's wealth wasn't really hurting him with the
voters at the end of his first year in office, though he was
vulnerable to the charge that he was making a power grab
with his demands for further control over state agencies.

The people did not particularly like Rockefeller as a person. He lacked the common touch, and to them he was an unimpressive leader. He was not one of them. He failed to relate to them or their problems.

But as he moved into his second year, Rockefeller seemed to be "talking much more to the point" than before. He began to handle himself more expertly on television. And the extreme divisiveness of the Democratic party worked to his advantage. Things were looking better. But a special session was coming. Fear in the Rockefeller camp began to spread. Special sessions were hazardous, could spin things out of shape.

In late March, 1968, things had slipped downward again. Nothing had been going right, it seemed. The approval level on the governor had skidded from 51 percent in late January to 32 percent two months later. This was the lowest reading so far. A whopping 59 percent of the people disapproved of the way Rockefeller was handling his job.

What had happened? It didn't take a seasoned observer to figure it out. A thirteen-day special session had just been concluded, and the public gave the nod to the legislature when asked about who was the more successful. Strife between the legislative and executive branches had surfaced decisively, and the public was beginning to be nervous and irritated by the constant snipping back and forth. Talk of a proposed tax increase didn't help matters; in a question to the people about the increase, 75 percent couldn't see the need to raise taxes. And discussion of a tax increase was particularly delicate in an election year.

Rockefeller had tried to offset the negative impact of talking about tax increases, traveling over the state in his "traveling office," a secondhand bus that was set up so visitors could be shuttled back to the rear for a brief visit with the governor, then out onto the courthouse lawn again. The governor thought these "regional visits," as he called them, were effective. The staff had mixed emotions.

He took somewhat dubious department heads with him on some of the bigger tours, and they agreed with the governor that the trips were worthwhile. But they didn't ask to go on others.

Rockefeller said he personally talked to 21,000 people on that summer's visits. But he said later that in spite of all the campaigning and public appearances he had seen comparatively few of his fellow Arkansans. Those who visited him in the bus were almost like people at a show—where you stand around for a few minutes, watching your neighbors go inside for a time and wondering what they're seeing; as they drift out the back door, seeming impressed, you shuffle forward yourself. "So many came," Rockefeller said, "and were a little bit awe-stricken. Sitting down relaxedly in the bus with pleasant people around and about, I don't think that awe lasted. Because of the numbers, I had to force them very quickly to coming to the point on what it was they wanted to talk about."[7]

Visits with the governor when his traveling office was parked in their hometowns were "as much symbolic to people as . . . rewarding." Rockefeller said the visits were rewarding to the townspeople because he wrote down what their problems were and when he got back to the capitol, problems on which action could be taken were delegated to the appropriate person and something was done about them. "I was trying to demonstrate to the people," Rockefeller explained, "that this was their government, not my government."

Rockefeller had warned the legislative council in April, 1968, that he wasn't seeking reelection as a "static, custodial governor." He also told them that "no knowledgeable and honest politician is going to be able to run on a 'no new tax' platform this coming summer and fall unless he, at the same time, admits to his constituents that even the minimum programs which we now have must be cut drastically."

WR sounded like he was scolding the legislators, implying that if they didn't vote more taxes they were dishonest. They didn't like it. The rift between the chief executive and the general assembly had widened so radically that by the time of the May session, a reporter wrote: "A person taking the few steps up the stairs from the Governor's office to the legislative halls last week was covering an appalling amount of ground. The distance between the governor and the legislature was far greater even than during the quarrelsome days of the regular session in 1967."[8]

At the second special session, May 20, 1968, Rockefeller again made some tax proposals. He called for three cents per package on cigarettes, which would yield about five million dollars annually. He said that the full impact of this tax wouldn't be felt immediately, nor would that of the tax he was recommending on mixed drinks. Noting that the tax on mixed drinks would involve the process of local option elections, he said that the cumulative effect "of our tax proposals can raise our revenues from $8 million to $10 million a year. This will enable us to extend our aid to education and to make the increased welfare grants that you and I originally planned."[9]

They would turn him down, decisively.

In a television address that same month, Rockefeller made no secret of his frustration with the legislators. He said their behavior the previous week "has been as disappointing to me as anything I have ever run into. The fun and games by some senators and representatives was supposed to be at my expense. They did hurt but that's a personal matter and I'll get over it. The real hurt is to you, the people. They know I'm right but it's more important to them that I don't get the credit. That's why they are carrying on this personal attack against me—to divert your attention and avoid coming to grips with the issue."[10]

Rockefeller said he had called the special session to make proposals for dealing with serious problems facing Arkansas. He described himself as a concerned but not a defeated man. He said he had done his best and that he had never claimed to be an experienced politician. "I've been criticized for my mannerisms, for the way I talk, for using complicated words, for my haircuts, for my boots, my hat, my airplane . . . just about anything else you can name. I've accepted this criticism in good faith and tried to improve myself by making use of constructive criticism." But, Rockefeller said, he wasn't worried about himself so much as about his program, which was designed to ease problems that some legislators were unwilling to face. "This is not a Republican program, it is not a Rockefeller program," he said.

> It's a program for the people of Arkansas. It proposes that we meet our promised salary increases to our teachers and that we provide money to colleges and universities to maintain sound programs for educating Arkansas' young people next year and to meet our present commitments. Hopefully, it will produce enough to allow modest welfare increases.
>
> Our problems won't go away just because some legislators are unwilling to face them. These problems will be here whether I'm governor or not and regardless of who is in the legislature. These problems must be faced and I say the place is here and now. The thing that upsets me is the eagerness to shoot down good and constructive programs purely out of political selfishness.[11]

The governor said he knew that his proposals would be controversial, but "progress is always controversial, because it requires doing something different in order to move ahead."

Still angered by the antics of the general assembly, Rockefeller said after adjournment that he wouldn't hesitate to recall it again, if necessary. The only meaningful fiscal bill passed might prove unworkable, WR said, and that would precipitate his calling a third special session. The bill to which he referred would take $2.3 million for state-supported colleges and universities. This would pull reserves down to $7 million, a figure the fiscal experts regarded as dangerously low. "I will not sign H.B. 25 but I may permit it to become law. Otherwise we may have no basis for operating our state agencies, meeting the commitments to the teachers and partially taking care of the prison problem."[12]

Did he dare hold another session in light of the shambles the lawmakers had made of his program in the one just ended? "I dare to do anything that's good for the State," Rockefeller replied. Branding the legislature fiscally irresponsible, WR rebuked the legislators for ignoring the state constitution and voting to increase payments to nursing homes with money from his contingency fund. "They chose in the waning moments of the session to further hamstring the governor by appropriating another one-half million dollars for the private business interests that operate certain nursing homes in the State of Arkansas."[13]

CHAPTER VI

Prison Reform

Rockefeller had scarcely moved from his election night headquarters to the governor's office before he was unceremoniously confronted with making a decision on a matter of impressive proportions: What to do about a lengthy state police report on brutality, extortion, murder, and sadism at the state prisons? This shocking report had been released prematurely by a Faubus aide. Rockefeller commented on the report at some length in his inaugural speech, pledging to improve the deplorable conditions immediately; but even he did not realize how bad the situation was.

WR handed copies of the report, with some names deleted, to the press, urging newsmen to use judgment and good taste in their handling of the explosive information. The new governor then turned his attention to correcting the abuses, knowing that both his staunchest supporters and his enemies doubted that his efforts would be successful. An attitude that he would find shared by an alarming number of Arkansans was that criminals should be confined and forgotten, that whatever happened to them, no matter how brutal, was what they deserved.

He told the Arkansas Press Association that he found in the state "a lack of righteous indignation" on the part of the people. Prison abuses were apparently something the people had grown accustomed to. His predecessor, Rockefeller explained, was proud of the profit made at the prison farm. But such profits were invalidated, WR felt, by the system's failure to rehabilitate the criminals—a theory supported by the number of prisoners who returned to the penitentiary repeatedly. The people of Arkansas, like people everywhere, believed that wrongdoers should be punished, Rockefeller acknowledged; but he didn't think that they should equate punishment with persecution.

Exemplifying the kind of political scheming that was rampant in dealings with the state's prison system is the following incident. Bob Scott, who served as the governor's aide on prison matters for most of the Rockefeller years in office, was approached by a Hot Springs deputy sheriff early in 1967. The deputy outlined to Scott his interest in a particular inmate who was serving a life term for murdering his wife. Scott, whose methods of operation embraced the practice of tape-recording conversations, recorded the man's spiel about getting his friend out of prison. The deputy was prepared to make a $1,500 campaign contribution to Rockefeller's next race in exchange for the prisoner's freedom. Although the governor's aide declined to accept this bribe, the incident does reflect the atmosphere in which WR's efforts toward prison reform were set.[1]

Two days after Rockefeller released the report on brutality at the prisons, he announced that he had no desire to see the prisons become a political football. He said there would be no finger pointing, that he wanted to sit down with prison officials and see what could be done. In an address to the general assembly in special session,[2] Rockefeller said:

> The people of Arkansas are scandalized by what they have recently learned about our penitentiary system. The solution is not an easy one. It involves, first, a definition of the system that we will have; second, it involves money; third, it involves sound planning. It is clear that the immediate investment will be substantial but with sound planning this need not be an excessive burden.
>
> By your actions at the last regular session, I believe you committed the people of Arkansas, once and for all, to a departure from the . . . archaic system of running our penitentiaries.

By tripling the number of free-world employees and by accepting the need to improve the food and living conditions of the prisoners, you recognized that we are phasing out the old approach. . . . However, at this time, I think it is necessary that we recommit ourselves, irrevocably, to a program of reform and I, therefore, urge you to enact into law the bill calling for the creation of a new Department of Corrections.

If he had any doubts about the difficulties he would encounter in overturning an evil system where some prisoners exercised the power of life and death over others, these doubts were dispelled by his first unannounced visit to the prisons early in his administration. The state police car in which he was riding was stopped at the gate by a convict guard. The governor was allowed to enter the prison only after the troopers had given their guns to the convict. "It's startling to have a convict disarm the State Police," WR observed wryly.[3]

Rockefeller, in a June, 1967, speech, said: "We have probably the most barbaric prison system in the United States. Some of the tortures that are inflicted on prisoners are beyond belief. Since I have taken office, we have started a variety of things moving. I hired for the first time in the history of the state a professional trained penologist. We have a Study Commission working on the long range problem of what kind of a prison system we want. We have a system where there were less than 28 paid people in our penitentiary system. Everyone else was an armed prisoner."[4]

Rockefeller fired four top officials at Tucker Intermediate Reformatory in February, 1967, on the basis of information his investigators had turned up among prisoners. "Pink" Booher, a former Jefferson County sheriff and assistant superintendent at Tucker, was among them. There had been reports that goon squads were operating at the prison, beating up some of the prisoners. The state police advised Rockefeller that the situation was critical and that for the safety of the personnel and the prisoners he should take immediate action to replace Booher and the others. After these firings the state police were put in charge temporarily. According to the officers, the way Booher ran the prison had many prisoners fearing for their lives; and fears for Booher's safety had also been voiced.

Rockefeller set out to find a reformer, a man whose dedication and ideals would carry him through the shattering first phase of overturning and reworking the whole system, a man tough enough to stand criticism and nonsupport from the legislature, one who could deal effectively with the prisoners running the prisons and could institute the different controls necessary for reform. Such a man he had found, Rockefeller thought, in thirty-nine-year-old Tom Murton. Brilliant and articulate, Murton began shaking things up from the day he arrived, including the administration. Murton's continuing stream of highly quotable criticism was not all well aimed; and his almost psychopathic disregard for channels of authority and for the need to get along with those with whom he must work soon had Murton and the administration in hot water with nearly everyone but members of the press, who loved the whole thing.

But there were those who believed, and still do, that a fire-breather like Murton was essential to getting the business of reform underway. Scott said Murton was the best thing that could have happened to prison reform, because he had the ability to get the average person interested in inmates, in convicts. Even with Murton there, though, it was obvious the people of Arkansas wanted to continue looking the other way. But Murton kept demanding their attention, until, with his revelations, there was a controversy. But before that point was reached Rockefeller would swallow more guff than he, in his most optimistic moments, would have believed he had the stomach for.

Rockefeller said on one occasion, "Murton's ego equals only his ability as a penologist." On May 22, 1967, Rockefeller was reported as "maintaining a stout defense of Murton." There had been criticism of a rise in the escape rate at Tucker, and Rockefeller answered, "We are doing the best we can with our resources." He went on to say that Murton had his full support "in what he is trying to do and how he is doing it." Privately, Rockefeller was already wondering if his prison program wasn't doomed with Murton. WR offered a mild rebuke to Murton, whose responsibilities were limited to the Tucker unit of the state prisons, for the penologist's comment to the press that most improvements at the Cummins unit, fifty-four miles away, were superficial and that the convicts still controlled the prisons. Rockefeller was irritated, but he still insisted that Murton was "doing an exceptionally fine job," adding that the state was in the midst of a prison study "and I do not know that a comment such as he made is going to help progress in the total prison system."[5]

Murton, who said Rockefeller had offered him the job of supervising both units, complained to the press about Rockefeller's criticism; and the governor observed, when the press asked him about it, that "Murton is a sensitive person. If I stepped on his toes, when I see him I'll apologize." And he did, in a well-publicized meeting at the capitol. Murton seemed mollified, and Rockefeller moved to promote him to heading both units.

The governor regretted this decision right away. Almost immediately after Murton moved into his new office he began digging at Cummins for bodies that prisoners had told him were buried there. And the publicity for this investigation, arranged for by Murton, was about as embarrassing as anything Rockefeller had encountered. Earlier, when Murton had told Scott that bodies were buried on the prison grounds, Scott had said, "Well, dig 'em up, dammit, and let's get some evidence of homicide." Scott said that, unknown to him, throughout the year, Murton had been digging at Tucker and had the grounds riddled with holes several feet deep. He found nothing there. The first thing Scott knew about any digging at Cummins was when he received a telephone call from Murton's secretary. She told Scott that Murton and others had just discovered bodies of murdered inmates. Scott took Lynn Davis, director of the state police, down to investigate. They found lots of media there. National television was already on the scene, filming—and at Murton's request. Indeed, the national television crew was there when the first spade was turned.[6]

Rockefeller said he didn't intend to become involved in prison affairs but that he was upset to learn through a newspaper article about the digging for bodies at Cummins. He criticized the state police for not keeping him informed. On February 9, WR said there would be no more digging for bodies until he gave the order. He said he had to be convinced that no legal complications existed before the digging was resumed; once he was satisfied that the administration was on solid legal ground, he would order the search for bodies in unmarked graves to continue. He said he was running out of patience with what he called decisions affecting the administration "made without my knowledge."[7]

The governor would later refuse to answer questions from a New York *Times* reporter who had been "in" with Murton from the beginning and had broken the story nationally. The governor wasn't willing to make Arkansas' prison problems a national publicity stunt. Even Murton, perhaps, could now see that he had given Rockefeller critics all the ammunition they needed for a full-scale assault on Rockefeller's prison reform progress and on Rockefeller himself, as well as on everything else Republican and different. The incident was disastrous, even though findings would ultimately demonstrate that the three skeletons found had apparently been buried forty years before, when the land was a paupers' cemetery.

In a speech to department heads in April, 1968, anticipating a special session, Rockefeller made these comments about the prison reform program:

> Until the General Assembly makes available to the new Department of Corrections the revenue necessary to finance the existing program and the expanded reform program which conscience dictates we must undertake, we cannot truly say that permanent prison reform has been effectuated in Arkansas. True, in the last 15 months, the people of the nation have witnessed a complete change in penal philosophy in Arkansas. The most important single change has been the recognition that inmates in our penal institutions are still human beings and regardless of their transgressions must be dealt with as children of God. While this fundamental change in philosophy is absolutely essential, it is not enough. To give meaning to the philosophy, we must provide the funds needed to establish the minimum conditions dictated by a program aimed more at rehabilitation than retribution. . . . We must move from the philosophy of prisons for profit to the philosophy of prisons for protection of our society.[8]

Murton's desire for power was augmented, not diminished, by all the controversy. Now that the post of state commissioner of corrections had been created, he wanted it. In fact, he said that Rockefeller had promised it to him. The governor concluded that it was time to close this particular chapter in prison reform. The media asked Rockefeller about his "promise" to Murton. WR responded that he wasn't sure Murton was the man he'd like to see in that job. Privately, Rockefeller was very sure. Murton knew it and kept talking to the media, this time in Berkeley, California, during what the governor felt was an unauthorized visit. Murton presented his position to the Californians and reviewed how lousy things had been in Arkansas until he took over.[9] "My patience," Rockefeller told the Arkansas media, "has worn thin." This was, perhaps, the understatement of the administration.

The governor wanted Murton thereafter to reply to questions about conditions at the prison before he took over with "no further comment." But Murton, who arrived at the Little Rock airport from the controversial Berkeley visit to greet the media in an impromptu news conference, was told that the governor was steamed about the California trip, that the chief executive didn't even know his prison superintendent was out of state.

Murton, playing to the standing joke about Rockefeller always being somewhere other than in his office, said it was quite possible the governor didn't know Murton was out of state. He hadn't known the governor was in the state. They all laughed. But Rockefeller was not amused. In fact, if a last straw had been needed, this was it. Rockefeller, who lacked the legal authority to fire Murton, prepared a carefully worded letter to members of the board of corrections, making it clear that he would be happy if they said goodbye to his choice, Tom Murton. They did, with apparent relief. Among the thoughts in Rockefeller's letter to the prison board were these:

> I might go further and state that not only are you under no commitment to appoint Mr. Murton to this position [as commissioner of corrections] but you are under no commitment to retain him in any position whatsoever in the Arkansas prison system. Although Mr. Murton has exhibited competency as a penologist, he is totally incapable of, and insensitive to, the requirements of operating in harmony with his associates in a governmental structure. The loyalty of his subordinates is impressive, but his callous disregard for the problems of his equals and his superiors has created a wholly untenable situation. The decision is yours but I believe you are entitled to know where I stand on this controversial issue. The progress we have made in prison reform, which started under my leadership, before Mr. Murton arrived in Arkansas, will be continued whether Mr. Murton remains or not. No individual is indispensable. As I see it, the question you are faced with is simply this: "Is Mr. Murton's continuing association with the penitentiary system in the best interest of the state and of our prison system? Reluctantly, I have finally concluded that my answer to this question is No."[10]

On March 8, 1968, John Haley, chairman of the state

board of corrections, produced a list of complaints against Murton that he said led to the abrupt decision to relieve him of his job. Haley said that he had hoped to avoid making the incidents public, but that public exposure was now unavoidable. He said Murton persistently overspent, despite warnings from the board; that he was repeatedly insubordinate, refusing to confer with board members before taking many actions and ignoring some of the board's decisions; that he circumvented state purchasing laws to obtain supplies faster; and that he addressed staff members and other state officials with sarcasm and contempt.[11]

Austin McCormick of New York, a penologist who had been a consultant for the state's penitentiary study commission in 1967, said that he did not discount Murton's ability, courage, and honesty. McCormick acknowledged that Murton had done everything he could to improve the dietary and living conditions and to see that all inmates were treated fairly. These improvements, however, did not qualify him for the top position, McCormick said. What disqualified him was his refusal to deal reasonably with legislators, budget people, judges, law enforcement officers, prosecutors, the press, the public, the governor and his staff, and the board of corrections.[12]

Murton told the United States Senate Juvenile Delinquency Subcommittee, on March 4, 1969, that the state of Arkansas had failed to back him up when he tried to "overhaul the degenerate system at its very roots."[13] Murton also described the Arkansas prisoners as possibly the worst in the world. He told his harrowing story of brutality and atrocities to the subcommittee, which was studying conditions in the nation's prisons. The subcommittee chairman, Senator Thomas J. Dodd of Connecticut, asked Murton if the tape recording of an alleged beating of a nineteen-year-old inmate that he played for the subcommittee (which he said was made secretly by another prisoner) was authentic. Murton vouched for it.

Rockefeller reacted angrily to Murton's testimony before the subcommittee. He called Dodd to tell him that the state would offer rebuttal testimony and would invite members of the subcommittee to visit the Arkansas prisons. Murton had told the subcommittee that he had been fired because he "dug up bodies of inmates I believe were murdered." Dodd said he would be happy to hear an Arkansas representative testify about conditions in the state's penitentiary system. Rockefeller sent the new prison superintendent, Robert Sarver; and the governor went on television to deny Murton's charges about prison conditions in Arkansas, branding them a complete fabrication. He explained that the conditions Murton described were conditions that existed prior to Rockefeller's taking office and that many of the problems had been corrected.

The difficulties in prison reform often were more political than penal, particularly during the campaigns of 1968 and 1970. For example, an electrifying television spot regarding abolishment of the strap at the prison was prepared for the 1968 campaign. It showed a hand raising the strap; and then, as words described its use, the strap was whipped down with the sound of hide on flesh. An actual recording of sounds made by some prisoners being beaten during an earlier administration was in the background. The effect was really dramatic and in some respects in bad taste. But that wasn't the reason the spot was never used.

Just about the time it was ready to go on the air, an incident occurred at the prison in which a trusty guard fired birdshot into a group of prisoners. The Rockefeller organization withdrew the strap spot immediately, convinced that the case for prison reform would not be advanced by impressing on people that the Rockefeller administration had moved from straps to shotguns in less than two years. No matter what the facts were in this case, it was too emotional to ask for logic and reason. Rockefeller aides decided people would understand the birdshot incident if the strap spot didn't appear simultaneously. With both things going at once—that is, news reports of the birdshot incident with the television spot featuring the strap—an overreaction to the prison situation might set in.

The prisoners were certainly aware that their champion was Murton. He defended them to a fault, some critics on the outside said; and it is safe to say they didn't view Sarver with the same affection they felt for Murton. The day before the Rockefeller-Bumpers showdown in 1970, eight inmates seized four hostages and threatened to kill them unless the prisoners were allowed to escape.

Sarver and Cummins superintendent Bill Steed tried to reason with the inmates and join the hostages. After holding the hostages for more than twelve hours, the prisoners surrendered. About seventy-five state troopers had gone to the prison, armed with shotguns and pistols, to get control of the situation. The prisoners yielded to the talk from Sarver and the threat outside, but Sarver made no deals. He said he wished some of the legislators could have been called down to the prison, because "it's a shame they couldn't live through something like that." Rockefeller praised Sarver later for his "character and his courage in resolving a very tense problem."

The uprising took place on the "punishment" side of the isolation unit—a white concrete block building behind the sprawling barracks complex at the prison farm. Some forty men were housed in the unit, half on one side for protective custody and administrative duties and the other half on the other side for punishment.

The inmates were armed with two 38-caliber pistols and a great deal of ammunition. The original four hostages were two civilian correctional employees at the prison and two trusty guards. The inmates first demanded a car, a tank full of gas, and time to escape. Later, when they realized they would not be allowed to escape, the inmates turned to complaints about such things as unsanitary conditions at the prison, inadequate kitchen utensils, lack of clothing, too many security shakedowns, and inmate guards firing their weapons too frequently while guarding other inmates in the fields.

Sarver said he had been notified at about 2 A.M. that maximum security inmates had taken hostages and had pistols and ammunition. He dressed and drove the seventy-five miles to the prison. He looked the situation over and decided that the governor ought to be told. He said the prisoners threatened several times to kill the hostages.

Later on that morning, the governor issued a news release that was read to Sarver over the phone, stating that the governor would not negotiate with the inmates, that no deals would be made. At the time the message was read to Sarver, he had already been taken hostage. Les Hollingsworth, then the governor's aide for prison affairs, had read the news release to Sarver. The whole affair, according to Sarver, simply underlined the need for what he called "a decent budget" for the prisons. But if he was looking for agreement among legislators that the rebellion pointed toward more money for the prison, he was badly mistaken. Senator Virgil T. Fletcher of Benton was quoted as saying, "It's a typical example of the era of excellence. . . . We didn't used to have things like that at the prison."

After the prisoners gave up, the state police devoted the next nine hours to a shakedown of the prison. They turned up some five hundred objects that could be considered potential weapons—including pliers, safety razors, tableware, a logging chain, a metal carton ripper with a short blade and a band to fit around the finger, a cutdown paring knife, a metal fork with the prongs bent out, eight clubs made of wooden handles, eleven pairs of scissors, nine files, four saw blades, and fourteen screwdrivers. There were some very ingenious weapons among the cache: a spoon handle sharpened into a shiv and two "sock clubs"—one containing a padlock and the other a bar of soap. The officers also found a .45 caliber shell, five rounds of rifle ammunition, and fifty-five .44 magnum shells. No guns were found.

Despite the difficulties encountered along the way, Rockefeller made significant changes in the area of prison reform. He outlawed the strap in punishment, stopped all torture and beatings, developing—as an alternative—isolation and disciplinary barracks and the revocation of good behavior time. In terms of security, he set up civilian guards to control work crews, isolation units, yards, and barracks. He began the task of replacing armed trustys as funds permitted and started developing a maximum security unit at Cummins.

He required a balanced diet for the prisoners, with milk and meat every day. Disinfected kitchens, isolation cells, and barracks were instituted, and clean bedding and linens were required. WR even began a pest control program. He put the infirmary under professional supervision at both units and channeled income from the prison's plasma program into better medical service.

In terms of agriculture, Rockefeller brought about crop controls and improvements. And he began mechanization of the farming operations.

WR stopped inmates from keeping records and assigning jobs, prohibited the use of prisoners or prison property for private gain, instituted a program for strict auditing, put professional penologists in charge, and brought about a dramatic change in the prisoner-to-staff ratio—from 58 to 1, the ratio became 8 to 1. He also began training programs for the prison staff.

The Rockefeller administration began classifying prisoners every three months as to security risk, job assignment, medical condition, and psychological condition. He

directed that young offenders be sent to Tucker Intermediate Reformatory and the older offenders to Cummins.
WR also carried out prison integration.

Rockefeller began academic classes at Tucker, and vocational training facilities were completed in both institutions. Sizable amounts of federal money were obtained
for education and rehabilitation. Inmate-run newspapers
were begun, a professional director for athletic programs
was retained, and a new chapel was built by private donations at Tucker. More than nine hundred inmates were
placed in jobs as a result of a new prerelease employment
program. Under the direction of Rockefeller, Arkansas'
four juvenile training schools were placed under one board
and consolidated into two desegregated institutions. In
1969, a diagnostic, evaluation, and classification center
was established and education programs were accredited
by the state department of education.

In a memorandum dated February 3, 1970, Eisele said
that for Rockefeller's peace of mind in the near and distant
future, "it will be necessary to commission a scholarly
book on prison reform in Arkansas which tells the true
story of Win's magnificent efforts in this area and which
refutes item by item and en toto Murton's unfounded
statements against Win, the penitentiary board members . . . and the new administration. Murton's paranoia
must be exposed and Win's record chronicled." [14]

CHAPTER VII

Reelection

You cut my throat," Charles Bernard said bitterly. He was talking to the two who had directed Rockefeller's successful bid for reelection—Bob Faulkner and me. The governor looked on in unsurprised silence. Bernard had asked for this meeting, and he wanted the governor there.

Against the governor's advice and the advice of his campaign staff, Bernard, a successful businessman from eastern Arkansas, had chosen to carry the Republican banner into a contest against Senator J. William Fulbright. His decisive loss was predictable—to everyone but himself. His anger and bitterness were also predictable. Many Rockefeller supporters were for Fulbright, and in more than one instance Bernard was able to show that Rockefeller campaign funds had been used to promote a Rockefeller-Fulbright-Humphrey ticket, mainly among blacks. Bernard resented the governor's role in his defeat, as did his supporters; and he had requested this meeting with the reelected governor and his two top campaign workers to air his feelings.

The scene was not atypical. Indeed, this incident was characteristic of the problems encountered by Rockefeller in the whole second-term election. WR had to keep Republicans happy and preserve his own political strength at the same time, while seeking to manage a government made up largely of Democrats with few qualified Republicans who could replace them.

Early in the year Bernard had sought out Rockefeller to ask his advice. What he really wanted was WR's encouragement and financial backing. But Rockefeller, through his campaign staff, had been hearing about polls, reading the political winds generally, and evaluating Bernard's candidacy. Could it hurt Rockefeller's chances? The answer seemed to be "yes." Many Rockefeller supporters were also Fulbright supporters, and a strong challenge to Fulbright would force many to choose whom they would work actively for. The net effect of it all would be that as Bernard gained strength, Rockefeller would lose strength.

So the decision was made: be nice to Bernard, but don't give him much help. That was all explained to Bernard. He accepted the decision, but went on and filed for the Senate seat anyway. Soon he was complaining that Rockefeller's organization was shunning him; and eventually he was enraged to learn that one segment of the Rockefeller campaign organization—a group of Democrats for Rockefeller trying to hang onto their Democratic credentials—was openly supporting Fulbright. Margaret Kolb, a leader in the Democrats for Rockefeller group during all the campaigns, said her organization had a poster of Fulbright and some buttons available, but they made no effort to promote him actively. "It was subliminal but it was so we'd ring true as Democrats nationally. And of course, deep down, a lot of us were supporting Nixon so we were a mixed up, very independent group."[1]

The Fulbright-Bernard race was viewed anxiously by the Rockefeller people from the beginning. It had within it the force to beat WR. Rockefeller's campaign staff didn't think that trying to talk Bernard out of running was being disloyal to the Republican party. It hardly seemed logical that the GOP could build on a lost political race, and the staff knew that Bernard wasn't right. He simply couldn't win; the polls and everything else suggested that. The Rockefeller organization's primary goal was to get Rockefeller elected, and there was no way Bernard's candidacy could help realize that objective. But it remained difficult not to alienate Fulbright people, who otherwise would be for WR, without angering good Republicans by not doing enough for Bernard. The defeated candidate did not understand or agree with the staff's view of the problem—not before or after his loss. And he left the meeting with Faulkner and me and WR more angry and frustrated than ever.

Rockefeller and his staff had been through their own unhappy moments, though the tension was easing. Late in July, 1968, there had been an apparent decline in the anti-Rockefeller feeling among voters. The opposition was taking shape, with Virginia Johnson (wife of WR's opponent in 1966) going down in a runoff against Marion Crank. Ted Boswell, a liberal young lawyer from Bryant, was defeated in the first primary. Had Boswell made the Democratic runoff instead of Mrs. Johnson, he might have defeated Crank and possibly Rockefeller. Nevertheless, Crank had won the Democratic nomination and he would be a tough opponent for WR. Good strategy called for visits to courthouses and talks with the "little people." By the first of September, the picture for WR was quite gloomy. "At the moment we would lose at about 60–40," the pollster reported from his new findings. Rockefeller wasn't told, since little would have been gained by his knowing the bleak figures. Anyway, he didn't ask about poll results much anymore.

Morale in the Rockefeller camp was low, but WR just wasn't going to march up and down those dusty roads again. Yet public support for him was steadily declining. He was never in his office, the voters said, was late for speeches too often, and too often appeared with a shot or two under his belt, giving the impression of a man who wasn't trying hard enough.

The campaign organization decided to stage a vigorous campaign opener to squelch those stories; and Winthrop, Arkansas, the beginning place for WR's other two openers, became the focal point of everyone's interest. Bruce

Streett, a public relations staff member, was called on to organize the event. Streett, a brilliant, flamboyant liberal who seemed able to get more work out of more people than anyone, took the wild idea of a train whistle-stop tour down across the face of Arkansas to Winthrop and made it work. It would be expensive—just how expensive nobody except perhaps Streett anticipated in the beginning—but it had great potential for lifting morale and getting the campaign started.

The first problem was getting a train. Missouri Pacific responded to the idea with what could only be called coolness. They didn't run passenger trains in Arkansas anymore, and they didn't take to the whistle-stop tour idea with any enthusiasm at all. There was only one man, the Rockefeller forces determined, who could stimulate the railroad's interest, and he was in the enemy camp. Bill Smith was a Crank supporter; but he was also the attorney in Arkansas for Missouri Pacific Railroad. Would he help? Smith took off his campaign hat and put on the other with dazzling swiftness, and in the bat of an eyelash, almost, MoPac allowed as how the train idea was going to be okay after all.[2]

Hopes were high for the success of the tour. Not the least of its attractions would be the capability for hauling a big crowd of WR supporters to Crank's home county. Whatever the expense, this was going to be worth it. Streett, with virtual carte blanche, even had the beat-up old Winthrop depot repainted; and he made certain that all the groceries in every little store that was within reasonable driving distance sold out almost to the walls, just so the merchants could wave a warm goodbye to this generous man in the cowboy boots. Ten thousand people showed up where five thousand were expected; the food ran out before the train, the longest passenger train in Arkansas in fifteen years, arrived with its eleven hundred hungry supporters (including forty reporters). The WR Campaign Special, twenty-one cars long, was assembled in Poplar Bluff, Missouri, and made its first stop in Arkansas at Corning. Governor and Mrs. Rockefeller boarded at Little Rock, and there was a whistle-stop speech in Hope to punctuate the glamorous trip, replete with folk and campaign songs, a jig danced by Dr. Gutowski, box lunches served by pretty girls in Rockefeller green dresses.

WR himself went through every car, shaking hands with the passengers. So did some of the other Republican candidates, though that wasn't planned. One who didn't shake hands all the way through was Ed Allison, a candidate for land commissioner. Allison was embarrassed and angered when one of the girls in Rockefeller green told him he couldn't campaign on the train, that it was WR's show.[3]

Despite its meager population of three hundred, Winthrop made a good show. Six thousand pounds of beef were consumed, along with twenty thousand soft drinks and a truckload of watermelons, as well as the contents of the neighboring grocery stores. Johnny Cash and his band entertained, along with some good Arkansas talent. And there was WR, the object of everyone's fascinated attention.

Perspiration clung to his forehead and lip. His seersucker suit was drenched; his handkerchief, a limp and useless swab he mopped across his face mechanically. It was a strain there beneath the big shade trees on that open stage, with only the microphone between him and the thousands of faces staring at him.

His condition—he knew it and they knew it—was the product of his indulgences of the past months. He had grown heavy, partly because he'd spent far too many evenings with drinks and conversations extending into the morning hours. Now he was before the voters, and the butterflies were flapping around in that commodious stomach with abandon. The shy man who was rarely seen in the governor's office—or in a lot of other places his critics and his friends thought he should be—was now on exhibition. What would he say?

He'd been fumbling and uncertain in recent public appearances. And his campaign crew was expecting—dreading—more of the same. When he journeyed to Winthrop, train and all, few held out much hope for WR to pull it off, either there or in the campaign to follow. Too much catching up was needed. But WR had some resources even he didn't know about, some reserves inside there with those butterflies. Those resources were somehow mixed with other chemistries that day in Winthrop, and they surfaced as WR faced the thousands of voters before him. He knew of their reasons for being there, many of them—free food, Johnny Cash, the whole carnival thing played out in a rural setting. But his speech captured them.

"I told you two years ago I would erase corruption and scandal in the prison system, and I did," he shouted at them. "I told you I would run out of the state the gamblers and racketeers, and I did. I told you I would run out insurance companies which were bilking thousands of our citizens out of their savings, and I did."[4] A political writer for one of the statewide newspapers wrote, "Governor Rockefeller emerged Saturday as a tough, hard-hitting candidate for reelection who will give no quarter to his Democratic opponent."[5]

When he'd finished the speech, the crowd was stunned. The people left with renewed hope and more than a glimmering of new respect for this man who had sweated and strained before them—a man wanting their support badly, asking and imploring. At one point the speech was punctuated with perfect timing by a pass over by WR's jet that was so low it sucked a bunch of balloons out of the top of an oak tree shading the listeners. When it was all over, someone touched off some fireworks—this wasn't part of the program—and Dale Enoch, a reporter for the Memphis *Commercial Appeal*, stopped to watch, pencil and notepad poised. He explained in mock seriousness as he got on the train that he fully expected the fireworks to spell out "Rockefeller for Governor" in wreaths of fire overhead.

Things looked better by mid-September. The opening had seemed to trigger that longed-for momentum. Meanwhile, there were signs that Crank's support was more tenuous than WR's, and hopes grew. By October, it looked as if 80 percent or more of the blacks would support WR, even though Wallace would carry Arkansas in the presidential race.

Rockefeller needed to be positive and forthright from here on. Everything pointed to the probability that a slashing campaign would fail. In mid-October, approval of Rockefeller's handling of the governor's office had skidded, disapproval was up. The electorate wanted political stability. Which man could provide it! The best strategy seemed to be one that would force Crank into a more defensive and intemperate stance. But it wouldn't be smooth sailing, not ever in the campaign. Sometimes Rockefeller himself saw to that.

For example, WR branded George Wallace a demagogue at just about the time the polls were showing that Wallace would probably lead the presidential ticket in Arkansas. When WR's staff asked him why he called Wallace a demagogue, the governor replied, "Because he is." The staff agreed, but the gratuitous remark created problems just the same.

Crank's forces had problems also, though, and that helped Rockefeller over the Wallace statement. Crank seemed to be at least half trying to cling to some support in the Humphrey camp. He apparently didn't want to put Rockefeller too much on the side of Humphrey sympathizers. For that reason he wasn't inclined to repeat Rockefeller's "demagogue" statement too often. After all, the Humphrey folks agreed with it.

But Crank wasn't so charitable with the governor's

comments about the need for more taxes, the possibility of a bond issue, the fact that he supported the idea of mixed drinks and had commented somewhat out of context about beer for eighteen-year-olds. All of these comments were bad news politically, and the organization did some real agonizing about how to contain their destructive potential. Crank knew he had something that cut across philosophies, and he tried to make the most of it. At this time in Arkansas, talk of increased taxes, not to mention changes in long-established attitudes toward alcohol, was not popular with the voters.

Rockefeller's campaign staff, already harried by various nonpolitical pronouncements and moves on the part of their candidate for reelection, feared the effects of WR's stand on these political issues. A campaign field worker wrote, on September 26, 1968: "It is becoming increasingly clear that statements made by Governor Rockefeller concerning bond issues and increased taxes for a means of finance for future projects in state government are taken with a very dim view by the people of south Arkansas. When he continues to hack away on these issues, he is losing votes. . . . I would suggest that we wait until the governor is reelected to talk about the bond issues and tax increases. To keep pounding away on this subject is political suicide."[6]

In late September, 1968, every move on the surface of the political waters was noted with fear and trembling by the nervous Rockefeller forces. A Rockefeller field man advised the staff that several disgruntled Republicans in the employ of Marion Crank were contacting borderline Republicans throughout the state in an effort to embarrass the governor with an organization called "Republicans for Crank." Circuit Judge Henry Britt of Hot Springs, no newcomer to the political arena, was one of those contacted. He considered attempting to expose the scheme but was not encouraged to do so.

Meanwhile, back in Little Rock, Orval Faubus had reportedly set up confidential headquarters with the goal of winning the sizable number of George Wallace supporters over to Marion Crank's side in the gubernatorial race. This incident reached almost comical proportions before it ended. Photographers climbed all over each other to get good camera angles from second-story windows nearby, and soon it was obvious—as several of the pictures illustrated—that the photographers had been discovered. Faubus defended himself by saying that he knew "Mr. Rockefeller's forces" had his setup under surveillance. The former governor branded it as an invasion of privacy "that is both reprehensible and unethical." Faubus referred to "a host of amateur Dick Tracys in the Rockefeller administration," saying that "the three sleuths" assigned to spy on him "are state employees, which is a misuse and waste of taxpayers' money."[7]

Faubus was scaring the Rockefeller organization a bit, by reinforcing their suspicion that the rising political star of the season was Wallace. In the Rockefeller camp, it became increasingly important to decide what must be done about the other Republican candidates, as well as about George Wallace and Fulbright. No one really had the answer, but the arguments—rising as they did from insecurity and fear—were long and damaging. The trouble didn't stop with three or four candidates or issues. The whole slate of Republicans, down to and including county-level candidates, had to be taken into consideration. Since Rockefeller's campaign staff included hardcore Republicans, lukewarm Republicans, plus some avowed Democrats who were going to serve as the vehicle through which WR money reached political aspirants, the arguments were as fierce as they were important, even when deciding among Republican hopefuls was the subject under discussion. But when some of the staff proposed to recommend support for some reform-minded Democrats who were running, things got sticky indeed.

Finally, the group agreed to oppose only four incumbent senators—all Democrats—and twenty-three house members. The legislative "program" to replace those who were certain to obstruct the governor's plans and the two-party system idea was a failure, at least in terms of how many legislators were replaced. None were, although a good deal of money was spent and time invested in mapping strategy for the mini-campaigns. Even the plan to back some reform-type Democrats led to success in only one or two instances. There were also the constitutional candidates on the Republican ticket to consider. Some of them had been recruited by the campaign staff for various reasons. Some staffers thought these candidates could win; others saw the candidates as illustrations of the GOP philosophy of offering the voters an alternative. Some thought none of the candidates could win and considered them nothing more than an expense and a nuisance. Still another view was that their being on the ticket validated the fact that a two-party system had indeed been born, and whether they were supported by the public in an enthusiastic way was of little consequence. At any rate, they were in the race (although a couple of them were definitely not the governor's choices), and the question of funding them needed answering.

The legislative candidates had bogged down from lack of exposure, the staff informed the governor; and more of that old cure-all—money—was required. Acknowledging that the decision was Rockefeller's, a memorandum from WR's staff referred to the governor's considerable investment of "money, time, leadership and energy . . . already devoted to the effort of building a second political party in Arkansas." Continuing, the memo said that "the amount of money we feel necessary . . . is minimal compared to that overall investment which you have already made."[8] This memorandum called for $198,000 altogether, but much more than that was spent before it was over. Although WR was somewhat reluctant to commit himself further, the logic of comparing how deep he was in already with a few more hundred thousand dollars was strong, and it prevailed.

The staff had met in a Little Rock hotel room to arrive at the joint recommendation contained in the memo. There was some angry debate over which candidate could win and which couldn't as the eleventh-hour (a month before election day) meeting continued. What finally evolved was a marvelous example of a peculiar sort of political naïveté. There were unapproved and uncoordinated promises and commitments to the candidates and their friends by individuals in the group, misguided intentions, internal competition, and an expansive generosity with someone else's money. The product was a different figure of money that ought to be spent for each of the five constitutional candidates.

If anything would divide the organization more than this fight over how much of the governor's money was going to which candidates, it was the question of how involved the Republican party should become in the Rockefeller effort. Some staff members didn't even want the other Republicans, particularly not Bernard, to display literature in the Rockefeller headquarters. Some members of the WR staff ultimately felt complimented rather than insulted at the bitter charge, "You're not a Republican!" Old partisan suspicions riddled the organization from top to bottom; WR and everyone else felt helpless to do much about it.

The Democrats for Rockefeller, for example, had been unpopular with the GOP since the day it was conceived. The hardcore Republicans just couldn't believe that this Democratic organization had been instrumental in WR's first victory and was vital to his efforts toward a second one.

The Republicans especially resented the favored treatment they saw the Democrats for Rockefeller receiving and the apparently ample funds being employed in their phase of the campaign. The GOP seemed to be relegated to a ballot-security role and other thankless but essential tasks, while the governor held press conferences with the Democratic group and appeared to be favoring certain high mogul Democrats that the GOP had been fighting ineffectively for years. GOP stalwarts felt that these big Democrats were just using WR, and they vented their anger, if not at the governor, then surely toward his political aides who appeared to be selling out the Republican party and all its candidates save one to guarantee the reelection of that candidate and his running mate.

Before it was all over, before WR had won his second term by a frighteningly close margin after starting 60–40 behind Marion Crank, the Republicans had turned much of their frustration on the governor's public relations office. But we had worked with Democrats as well as Republicans, and we seemed to have better responses from the former.

The Rockefeller organization was handed a ready-to-go negative issue in the last six weeks of the campaign. And Rockefeller's opponent handled the matter ineptly. Crank's family, including his eight-year-old daughter, had been on the state's payroll while Crank was in the general assembly. Documentation of this information had been produced by supporters of Boswell, the Democratic candidate who was defeated in the primary. His top aide, Warren Bass— who then joined forces with Rockefeller—brought the material with him. It was so easily come by that the Rockefeller organization was undecided about how to use it. Some wanted to use it early, to undermine Crank's credibility. Others wanted to wait and drop it late in the campaign so that it would be fresh in everyone's mind when they got to the polling place. Some didn't want to use it at all.

As campaign director, I decided to bring out the material

near the end of the campaign. But, in an attempt to blunt the effectiveness of this volatile campaign issue, Crank opened the subject himself in a statewide television address October 8. He said he was announcing the fact "so the Republicans can't make a big fuss about me putting my family on the state payroll."⁹ Thus, rather suddenly, there was no decision to make. We simply had to get the material out in as documented appearing a form as possible and try to ride it until election day.

The "Family Plan," as we called it, noted that Crank had taken "unusual" advantage of his position in the legislature over a period of years. Warrants and other public documents on file indicated that in 1963 Mr. Crank and members of his family had received $6,838 from the state, in addition to his regular legislative salary of $1,200. Included on state payrolls were two daughters, eight and fourteen, and a son, eighteen, who was reportedly a student at the University of Arkansas while he earned $612.90 as sergeant-at-arms for the house.

Crank's staff was insistent that he refute the "Family Plan" stories before they damaged him irreparably. Thus Crank went on television on October 15, 1968, in an attempt to handle the matter. He said that Rockefeller had charged and the news media had carried stories about Crank's relatives being employed during sessions of the general assembly. Crank said this was true, that there had been no effort on his part to conceal the matter. "In fact, I mentioned it before Mr. Rockefeller did. Furthermore, the matter is a public record." Crank said the most attention was given the employment of his daughter, Elizabeth, who was only eight years old. "The job she had was one she could do. An eight-year-old girl or boy can carry messages and work in the house just as well as an eighteen-year-old or an adult. Moreover, Elizabeth is acquainted with most members of the House. Certainly, she was glad to earn the money. She needed it, too, as did other members of my family who worked. This is something Mr. Rockefeller cannot understand. Certainly, Mr. Rockefeller never had to accept employment in his whole life and the same would be true of his children. None of them has ever had to worry about earning money with which to buy clothes or school supplies. Neither could I afford to send my children to an expensive private school in Switzerland as Mr. Rockefeller did with his son."[10]

Crank then launched into an attack on Rockefeller's hiring of Tom Murton to run the state's prisons and then overlooking or approving Murton's hiring his kinfolks to work with him. Crank mentioned others who had family on the payroll: Britt, whose brother worked in the revenue department; George Nowotny, Republican state representative whose secretary was employed on the house payroll; Jerry Thomasson, the GOP candidate for attorney general, whose wife was on the payroll while Thomasson served in the general assembly in 1963; Cynthia Houchin, who was carried on the payroll of the department of correction as a warden at the state prison at $400 per month while she was the personal secretary of John Haley, Rockefeller's appointee to the prison board.

But Crank's big mistake was mentioning the "Family Plan" at first in only general terms. As the story unraveled in bits and pieces week after week, it did more damage to Crank's image. Had he told it all at first, it would probably have died by election day.

Crank also responded poorly to WR's big campaign mailer—a magazine of photos and text entitled "Building for the People." It was a summary of Rockefeller's accomplishments during his first term, filled with photographs documenting WR's achievements. Crank took to television, after the booklets had been mailed statewide, to attack the mailing piece. Rockefeller's people chuckled at the mental picture of thousands of Arkansans heading for their wastebaskets to retrieve and examine, this time seriously, the material Crank seemed to regard so seriously. Waving the booklet angrily in a thirty-minute telecast, calling it "pretty good reading if you like fiction," Crank said it cost "hundreds of thousands of dollars" and was printed out of state besides. He charged that the booklet typified Rockefeller's administration "through its half truths, omissions and outright lies."[11] But Rockefeller's opponent succeeded only in a waste of his money, since the telecast did little more than provide some good notice for the publication.

The so-called "great debate" now occupied the attention of everyone. Rockefeller—quite early, before his opponent was nominated—had suggested that a debate of the issues might be in order. When Crank felt he needed the exposure, he proposed to meet Rockefeller, and television stations quickly responded with offers of free prime time. Letters from Rockefeller's supporters began to pour in to the campaign headquarters, urging that the governor not debate Crank. Various reasons were offered but the truth was—and some WR friends stated it frankly—WR's supporters didn't think their man would do so well. In fact, they felt fairly sure that he would come off poorly because of his sometimes rambling style in contrast to Crank's experienced debating skills, honed to a fine edge in many a legislative wrangle.

Some, maybe most, of the staffers didn't voice their opinions too freely, but they also felt Rockefeller might come off second best in a direct confrontation with Crank, especially if WR wasn't really up to par. But Rockefeller chose to accept the challenge, agreeing at the same time to go along with the imposition of some rather stringent guidelines that his staff developed to minimize the risks.

As the correspondence and telephone communications over the debate guidelines began, the Crank camp urged a free-wheeling argument, while Rockefeller's aides sought to have the debate so structured that there would be no possibility for the unexpected. And the Rockefeller folks went a step further. It was no secret that both camps had friends in the other. A couple of Rockefeller's aides—Charles Allbright and I—prepared a blistering personal attack on Crank and let a Crank partisan get it as WR's opening statement. Of course, Rockefeller knew nothing of this bit of subterfuge and had no intention of delivering such a speech, but the Crank folks apparently took it seriously. Without knowing what Crank was planning to say before the fake Rockefeller remarks were purloined, Allbright and I watched and listened gleefully as Crank seemed to base his opening on what he thought Rockefeller intended to say.

Just before the telecast, the Rockefeller staff went even further. They set up a large cheering section outside the studio. When WR arrived, the crowd waved signs and cheered vigorously. Crank was reportedly furious. He started off the debate mad, with a sour face that didn't improve a lot as the hour-long, formalized "discussion" went by, with WR doing very well indeed.

WR's harshest friendly critics judged it a draw, at worst. The Crank folks, counting on their man cutting WR to pieces, were disappointed. Meanwhile, the polls that had shown WR trailing Crank badly kept improving for WR. Newsom forecast a 51 to 49 percent victory for Rockefeller. And that's just about where it was when all the votes were in.

WR, Leona Troxell (a prominent Republican leader), and J. William
Fulbright at a political picnic during the 1968 campaign.

The governor in a parade in Springdale, during the 1968 campaign.

WR meeting with a group in his conference room at the state capitol i
April, 1968.

WR is presented a Bible by Waymon O'Neal, an inmate at Tucker Prison.

Courtesy *Pine Bluff Commercial*

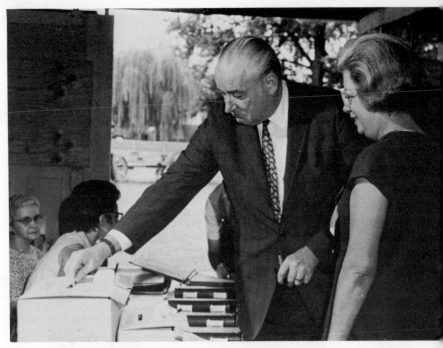

WR votes with Jeannette on primary election day, 1970, at Oppelo (near Winrock).

WR crosses a picket line at the Marion Hotel, where he and an assistant United States Labor Department secretary were scheduled to appear.

Ben Mitchell, chef and friend to
Rockefeller, at his kitchen desk at
Winrock.   Courtesy Ben Mitchell

The 1970 campaign helicopters, whose noise irritated neighbors near
the mansion.   Courtesy *Arkansas Gazette*

WR stands on the steps of the plane with his son, Winthrop Paul, after exploratory surgery in a New York hospital.

CHAPTER VIII

The Second Term

After the victory, Rockefeller began assessing the chances for passage of his tax package and some other reforms. The general assembly was going to be hostile and difficult. WR's opposition to incumbent Democratic legislators had not been well received.

The governor told the legislative council that a tax base should be provided which would make available about $15 million "over and above operating requirements" to meet certain capital needs. If no bond issue was approved, Rockefeller said, then there would at least be some funds available to meet critical needs in terms of capital improvements. "That Arkansas can handle this is not seriously in question," he said. "The question is with our pride in our great state. Are we willing to put our money where our mouth is? I believe we are." WR warned that if additional revenues were not produced, cutbacks would be necessary, cutbacks in welfare payments and teacher salaries. Enrollment in colleges would have to be restricted, and the outpatient program for the care of mental patients would be lost. Such things as penal reform and aid to the retarded, the blind, the deaf would also come to a halt if the minimum programs he proposed were not enacted.[1]

Rockefeller took to television in late November to request public support for the tax proposals which he'd be presenting to the general assembly later.[2] He had talked about them in rather general terms during the campaign, but now he would begin to be more specific. He offered an estimate, which would later prove somewhat short, of

$65 million per year that the state would need in order to "upgrade services" that were needed and to add new programs that would keep Arkansas "in step with the rest of the nation." He immediately turned then to private luncheons and conferences with business and professional leaders and some legislative friends to build a base of support for his fiscal program.[3]

In an appearance before the Arkansas Legislative Council on December 10, Rockefeller became quite specific, telling the lawmakers his program would produce $90 million the first year in new revenue (if passed by the legislature) and $105 million the next. He outlined some of the revenue producers he had in mind—hiking the sales tax, hikes in personal and corporate income taxes and cigarette, tobacco, and alcoholic beverage taxes, along with a reexamination of "each present source of revenue and all possible new sources of revenue."[4]

Next, sessions were organized for groups of guests invited by the governor, members of his staff, and state officials. A December 13 session was staged to "sell" the tax program and its benefits with speeches to organizations, group resolutions, letters to newspapers, and widespread use of stickers bearing the campaign slogan "Arkansas is Worth Paying For."

Thus would he try to counteract the coolness with which his proposals were received by most legislators. There were some pretty big business types at the December 13 session, among the 225 persons attending. Among them were William E. Darby, chairman of the commission on higher education financing; State Police Director Ralph Scott; Corrections Commissioner Robert Sarver; Gerald Fox, Fayetteville city manager; A. Allen Weintraub, administrator of St. Vincent Infirmary, and Ray Widmer of the planning commission staff. All these and several others made presentations designed to help convince those at the meeting and the public in general of the critical need for more funds.

The vast scope of the program was one reason it needed selling. A 1 percent sales tax increase, from 3 to 4 percent, and higher income tax rates on middle- and high-income families and corporations were at the base of the program. A rebate system for families whose annual income was less than $1,020 per member was proposed to offset criticism that the sales tax would hit low-income families hardest.

In late December, WR was quoted as saying he would take the "social" approach to softening up the legislators, mostly still unconvinced about his program. He would entertain them in groups of twenty at Winrock Farms, he said, prior to the start of the legislative proceedings on January 13.[5]

In January, the Arkansas Citizens for Good Government, which included several prominent businessmen, was formed to promote the need for and value of increased state income. Herbert L. Thomas, founder of First Pyramid Life Insurance Company and chairman of the group, said it endorsed "the spirit" of the governor's tax program. Chairmen were named for each county; these men spoke to various groups, supplying facts and figures about state government. Meanwhile, Rockefeller himself talked with business, professional, and civic leaders around the state. A few legislators yielded just a tiny bit, and on January 26, several, a newspaper account stated, said they liked "Mr. Rockefeller's $100 million a year program," but they doubted the public wanted to pay the necessary taxes for it."[6]

By February, rival bumper stickers bearing the slogan "Is Rockefeller Worth Paying For?" had appeared. Some were personally distributed by Senator Guy H. "Mutt" Jones of Conway, who also had one on the wall behind his desk in the senate chamber. At one point Jones repeatedly altered one of the stickers to read, "Arkansas Is Paying for WR." Before taping a television speech urging support of his tax program, Rockefeller was asked to pose with one of the rival stickers for a newspaper picture. WR managed a broad smile for the photograph, quipping, "Someone tell me a real funny joke so I can be laughing about this."

In December Rockefeller had told the legislative council: "Although my victory in the minds of some may not be considered a mandate in running for increased taxes and emphasizing the need for a bond issue, I violated the tradition long since established by far more experienced politicians than I. The fact that I stand before you today as your reelected governor is proof that a substantial majority of the people have, as do I, confidence in our future." The newly reelected governor asked the legislators to "employ guts, vision, understanding and a spirit of bipartisanship."[7] The councilmen didn't like that; nor did they like his claiming that his reelection was proof that a majority of Arkansans supported increased taxes and a bond issue.

In his second inaugural, on January 14, 1969, Rockefeller said:

> I am happy and proud that under the leadership of the first Republican governor in 94 years the 66th General Assembly enacted more legislation than any to go before it and that I signed this record amount of legislation into law. I would show less than my usual candor were I not to acknowledge at the same time that we may also have had a record amount of theatrics and horseplay leading up to the passage of this legislation. But the fact remains that Arkansas is indebted to the 66th General Assembly for much wise and constructive legislation, and this new legislation is moving us forward toward that Era of Excellence I have spoken about so often.
>
> I am angered when I hear it implied that because I and my family are blessed with material things it is easy for me to make bold proposals. Nothing could be further from the truth. My family was blessed with something infinitely more important; with compassion and a deep sense of obligation to others. So long as thousands of our people go to bed hungry or in hopelessness every night, nobody in Arkansas, myself included, has the right to be callous or indifferent.

If my blessings were only material, I would not be here today, in the role in which I am here.

There are no frills in what I am proposing, no luxuries, no monuments to me as an individual, as some have characterized what I am trying to do. If dreams are involved in my thinking, they are relative only to the nightmares—to the way of life—of those who, with enough compassion and courage on our part, could be helped to help themselves. Let each of us in a position of leadership, either elected or otherwise, be honest enough and courageous enough to admit one thing now:

To be influenced in our decisions by vocal and selfish people and resist these necessary fiscal reforms, is indefensible leadership, and it betrays those we represent. I implore every member of the General Assembly as I have myself: Listen to the voice of the people, not to the selfish interests, and ask God's help that our conscience will clearly distinguish between the two.

Who will provide the leadership? I will.

Who can get the job done? You can.[8]

The most vociferous detractors of Winthrop Rockefeller will admit that the Arkansas legislature came to know and enjoy an unparalleled independence during the years of his governorship. WR's tenure was very different from that of his predecessor. Orval Faubus as governor had typically told the assembled lawmakers that if they didn't support his road program he would assume they didn't need any roads in the districts they represented. Messages from Governor Faubus were just that clear, just that threatening, and legislators who hoped to be reelected responded affirmatively to virtually anything Faubus asked. One of the state's best-known political cartoonists, George Fisher, created a classic panel depicting those rubber-stamp days. He drew a caricature of Faubus addressing the legislature. Every person at every desk looked exactly like Faubus. Even the pictures on the walls and a mouse beneath the lectern bore the visage of the chief executive.

Things wouldn't be that easy for Rockefeller. His attempts at threatening the legislators were in vain. WR simply didn't have the political power that Faubus had. He couldn't hurt the lawmakers politically and they knew it.

The fighting became increasingly intense as Rockefeller tried to push for approval of his proposals—proposals that the legislators came to view as too farfetched, too expensive, too controversial, or just too "Rockefeller." If the man on the second floor was for it, then the men in the house and senate were going to be against it.

But despite the enmity between Rockefeller and that legislature, the record of reforms achieved during the Republican governor's tenure in office excelled that of any previous four-year period in the state's history. In his first term Rockefeller secured the passage of 741 acts. The second term would prove even more productive, with a total of 885 acts being passed before it ended.

One of WR's first moves in his second term was designed to demonstrate to the legislators that he had no hard feelings toward them. He invited the lawmakers to bring their wives and join him and the first lady at Winrock Farms for a restful overnight visit and some serious business as well. The governor hoped to show them that it was a new day, that he was of a forgiving nature and hoped they were.

But after the legislators came and went, and while the governor was enjoying the prospects of a productive legislative session, the Winrock staff prepared a report that would require more forgiveness from WR. The report itemized the number of Winrock towels, washcloths, perfume, cologne, hair dryers, extra toothbrushes, table decorations, pens, and the like that had gone home with some of the legislators. Rockefeller, who controlled his temper for the most part, was furious. He seriously considered submitting an itemized bill to the legislature. Later, he could joke about the $3,000 worth of "souvenirs" the guests removed from his home: "I'd have to say they enjoyed my hospitality and wanted to remember it."[9]

The governor returned to the capitol determined to do as much as he could for his program. He kept talking about large tax increases, about programs as visionary and worthy as they were impossible to get past the legislators who were convinced that WR was a lame duck for sure this time (hadn't Rockefeller said he wanted only two terms?)

When he addressed the joint session about half way through the first 1969 session, Rockefeller was testier than usual. He said he found two attitudes prevailing toward his program. One was impatience with him and the other a sort of persistent inertia represented by the idea that "Rockefeller hasn't demonstrated any real needs." Rockefeller said he was weary, but he was not ready to give up. He reminded the legislators that he had not sought reelection dishonestly—promising no new taxes yet pledging progress for Arkansas. He had admitted in his campaign for reelection that meeting Arkansas' needs would cost money, and he believed that his success offered proof that the people of Arkansas were aware of these needs and wanted them met.

Rockefeller again listed the problems and then said: "Needs? Some of us may be tired of hearing about them. Others because of political myopia may not yet have got around to recognizing them. But, yes, the needs are there. The question before us is whether to leave the needs alone and allow them to become the permanent character of Arkansas, or to meet these needs headon and enjoy a growth such as we have never seen before." The governor continued:

> It is good that in providing brick and mortar we have indicated an important concern for the education of our children. But sound education grows not from brick and mortar alone. Our faculties are underpaid. Our library shelves are understocked. Our science labs are underequipped. Our classrooms are inadequate, crowded and under great stress because of the needs of more and more students. Shall we now with a show of hands decree each institution to be a full-fledged university? Shall we expect handsome new signs at the front gates? And fancy new letterheads? Knowing that we have not provided the funds even for these niceties, then, turn away with false pride

to let mediocrity and worse eat away at the very heart of these institutions that must determine the ultimate quality of our social order? What price for such pathetic pursuit of responsibility? [10]

There was no surge of sentiment in favor of higher taxes, but by January, 1969, there was a noticeably greater tolerance, even resignation, toward the necessity for an increase. The climate of Arkansas public opinion was more favorable by then than it had been for many years in regard to raising taxes for purposes of general improvement and extension of state service. Confidence in the Rockefeller administration had increased also. Approval of the way the governor had been handling his job had risen to 48 percent, and disapproval had dropped to 30 percent.

But during the legislative session, public attitudes toward Rockefeller's tax increase proposal cooled. The 25 percent who one month before had said his proposals were justified as a whole had dwindled to 14 percent; and although the percentage saying the program was justified in part had risen from 55 to 65 percent, the total of the two bodies of opinion was about the same. Rockefeller wasn't winning the battle in public opinion, even though he had committed a considerable amount of his own personal funds to the statewide effort to rally public support. He had to admit it. The "Arkansas Is Worth Paying For" campaign had failed. Indeed, the effort seemed chiefly to be informing people that an attempt to raise taxes was underway, with the result that more and more of them fell into the ranks of those against such a movement.

Rockefeller addressed the joint session again on March 10, 1969, and his speech was filled with resignation that his program would not pass. He was concerned that something, however minimal, be approved so that the session would not have been in vain:

Thank you for allowing me to speak to you in joint session again. I wish it could be in happier circumstances. Unfortunately, we have a problem, a mutual problem. I am here in the hope that we can work together to solve it. I have proposed a program that I believe will meet Arkansas' needs. You have not enacted it.

You have said "no" to my program. I must now respectfully ask what is the alternative?

Rockefeller asked the legislators for two things: time for making decisions on a minimum program by calling a two-week recess, and that committees be appointed to work with the governor and his staff during the recess. Near the end of his speech he said:

You have heard comment about a possible third term. Let me say for the record here and now that I do not seek a third term as governor, but I do feel a responsibility to press for the re- forms for which I sought reelection. I have willingly invested several years of my life in this cause, and if I must seek a third term to finish my job then I will. I have tried hard to make my case with you. To date I have not succeeded. I am still trying and I will keep trying. I believe we can find common ground before it is too late.[11]

The major elements of WR's program broke down this way: elementary and secondary education, $15.5 million; higher education, $14.5 million; social welfare, $12.3 mil- lion; health services, $9.2 million; cities and counties, $10 million; resource development, $5.4 million; law and order and public safety, $10 million; tourist development, $2.2 million; and capital requirements, $15 million. Among the measures the lawmakers approved in WR's second term were taxes on cigars and some other tobacco products, an increase in the beer tax, and a real estate transfer tax. They raised the motor vehicle operator's license fee to six dollars for two years, removed certain tax exemptions from public transportation and communica- tion companies and utilities, increased retail and whole- sale liquor and beer permit fees and native wine tax, in- creased tax on cigarettes, increased the income tax on domestic and foreign corporations, and imposed a tax on timber land. The legislature also created a department of mental retardation at the governor's request, passed a bill authorizing mixed drink licenses if approved in city or county referendums, established a personnel classification and compensation plan for certain state agencies, and provided for a constitutional convention by setting a date.

Rockefeller said the public would probably remember this 93-day session (the longest in Arkansas history) for three things: the mixed drink law, the merger of Little Rock University with the University of Arkansas, and the $20 million raised in taxes. That $20 million wouldn't be enough, the governor repeated after the failure of the major bills that would have increased personal income tax and state sales tax and extended sales tax to include services. But it was a start.

Public agreement with the legislature—that taxes should be increased but not nearly so much as the governor wanted—was an overwhelming 89 percent. Support for Rockefeller's larger plan was 24 percent. In October, 1969, Rockefeller had very nearly the same popular approval level of six months earlier. Two months later, he was still being rated high by the voters surveyed. His popularity rested largely on his record of providing tangible and valuable new opportunities, a record that would be one of the significant accomplishments of his administration.

But there remained strong reservations among the public about WR's desire to increase revenues in order to provide more and better state services. The people wanted improved services and broader opportunities, but they didn't want to pay for these gains with additional taxes. This inconsistency would be one of the paradoxes that frustrated Rockefeller throughout his tenure. He would never understand it.

Rockefeller called the legislature back into session and addressed the joint session on March 2, 1970. He said he had received lots of advice—most of it warning him of the political peril inherent in calling another session. "I wish just one had told me how, in good conscience, I might not call you here and still live with myself," he said. He identified crisis items that he thought justified calling the session, some other matters that he called emergency items, and some housekeeping problems that needed the legislators' attention.

Rockefeller recalled that in December of 1968 he had presented to the legislative council what he believed were the courses of action then open. The one best course, a course of rapid progress, was a program that required $90 million in new revenues. His feelings had not changed, he said; he still believed strongly in that program. "But conceivably, my confidence in it has exceeded my powers as a salesman." At the other extreme was an alternative unacceptable in his view—a regressive, unplanned program calling for $20 million. That program, he said, would solve nothing; it would merely pay the bills at the rate they were coming in, and with costs rising it would not even allow the state to hold its own. At the top was the $90-million plan for rapid progress; at the bottom, $20 million for certain deterioration in the quality of government.

"It is to the middle course that your administration is dedicating its efforts now," the governor told the assembled group. "A program identifying $60 million in needs. You provided $20 million in our last meeting here. I am urging you now to provide the balance."[12]

As the prospects for any success in this session waned, Rockefeller became more critical of the preceding session, telling the Republican state committee that the legislature was "retrogressive," and that its whole purpose was "to clip the authority of the administration. They did not even have the courtesy to debate the measures," Rockefeller said. He seemed unable to recognize or believe that the lawmakers didn't care whether he could justify his program.[13]

Uncharacteristically, the governor even lashed out at the press after this disastrous session, asserting that the media ignored the value of his recent trip to Washington on behalf of several projects in Arkansas. Newsmen, he said, had preferred to concentrate their attention on the disaster his program had suffered at the hands of the legislators. "I came back from Washington recently during the special session and there was nothing in the press about what I was doing in Washington, but there was a big headline: 'WR's program a flop.' "[14] Rockefeller had made a number of contacts in Washington that he felt were valuable for Arkansas.

In an editorial that began by saying "Governor Rockefeller has had a bad week," the columnist went on to describe one of the chief executive's speeches as "largely incoherent."[15] But the governor, coherent or not, firmly believed the voters would replace half the legislators in the 1970 election because of their defeat of his tax program.

A month after the abortive session of the legislature, opinions and attitudes were beginning to take shape. They were ominous. Approval of the governor had dropped 11 points since December. (WR had not yet made his intentions known, but it was generally believed that he would seek a third term.) Particularly disconcerting to Rockefeller's staff was the result of an April, 1970, survey. Support for WR among blacks had declined dramatically, with only half of them saying that he should run again. Among all voters, 36 percent wanted to see WR elected to a third term; 49 percent did not.[16]

But the public was becoming resigned to the inevitability of some tax increases. Two out of three were now saying that the state might need some more revenues in 1971. The people were beginning to see, however grudgingly, the governor's logic about the need for upgrading state services to keep pace with the times.

However, the chief concern of the Arkansas voter was that he wanted more stability, less dissension. Voters were not so much opposed to Rockefeller as they were fearful that he might never be able to bring harmony between the executive and legislative branches of government. Rockefeller himself was respected, even praised for his efforts by many voters; but many of these same voters did not think he could succeed with a recalcitrant legislature. What these voters wanted was an explanation, simple and clear, of what needed to be done and how to do it, pollster Newsom reported—how to repair that bridge, to throw a line across the chasm between the Republican governor and the Democratic legislature.

CHAPTER IX

Years
of Reform

The true reformer, according to Tom Murton, must accept each challenge with the knowledge that ultimately he would be consumed in the process. If Rockefeller had any fear of being "consumed in the process" of reform, he didn't evidence it.

Almost every day of the Rockefeller years, something was going on to change things. Rockefeller looked for chances to tear down the old and build the new. At times, many felt he overstepped his authority in pursuit of his objectives. He perhaps lost more battles than he won, but he either set the stage for reform or achieved it in many areas—insurance, alcoholic beverage control, governmental efficiency, game and fish management, stock investment regulation, freedom of information. He was able to restrict political contributions with strings (more like heavy chains) attached and to drive away party leaders and functionaries with their hands near or in the till. Improvements in penology and race relations as well as imposition of some needed taxes were among his accomplishments. Rockefeller was, of course, harshly criticized for presuming to involve himself in the sacred institutions of Arkansas, but he persisted.

In January of 1967, a suit was filed in Pulaski County Chancery Court requesting an order to stop the Arkansas Loan & Thrift Corporation (AL&T) from representing itself as a bank trust company or savings and loan association. That was the first step in a slow but eventually successful move to shut down this company which existed under false and corrupt pretenses. In September of 1968 Federal Judge John A. Miller ordered liquidation of the firm and its subsidiary company, so that the two thousand depositors might collect whatever was left of their savings. The corporation's liabilities exceeded its assets by about $3.2 million. The names of several well-known politicians were among the organizers and inside stockholders of the company. Among those losing money in the organization were two churches in Booneville, as well as some cemetery associations that had invested money.[1]

Faubus was never directly linked to the scandal, but it became clear later that he had been urged to act against it, or at least investigate it. When Joe Purcell succeeded Bruce Bennett in the office of attorney general, he immediately filed a lawsuit against AL&T. John Norman Harkey, an aggressive attorney from Batesville and the new insurance commissioner, was also committed to insurance reform; he sent the AL&T house of cards tumbling when he ruled that Savings Guaranty Company, insuror of AL&T deposits, didn't have sufficient assets to supply the protection it claimed to have for the AL&T deposits.[2]

Eventually the AL&T case reached Judge Miller's court, and he declared the company insolvent. He ordered assets of it and two affiliated companies distributed to the depositors, who eventually got back roughly 60 percent of their investment. Many were indicted in the scandal, including Bruce Bennett. Several were convicted and served prison terms, but Bennett's trial was delayed because of illness.

On May 20, 1977, the 27-count indictment against the former attorney general was dismissed.[3] Reasons given by United States Attorney Robert Johnson in asking Judge Oren Harris for the dismissal were Bennett's poor health and difficulty in locating possible witnesses. The charges had been pending since January 30, 1969. "I'd like to thank my friends and attorneys for their continued faith in me," Bennett said as he left the federal court.

The "Game and Fish controversy," in which Rockefeller

sought to remove some of the commissioners for what he considered a flagrant abuse of office, is another example of his determination to change things and the correspondingly determined resistance to change that he faced repeatedly. The conflict began quietly enough. Joe Gaspard, a GOP fieldman, was denied access to expense vouchers, bid records, and cash receipts for the sale of surplus equipment by the Arkansas Game and Fish Commission. Gaspard's requests were passed off by the commission as "harassment" and nothing more.[4]

The new Republican governor, who had been hearing reports for months about wrongdoing in the Game and Fish Commission, was ready to take action. He drafted a letter of protest to all commission members, expressing his disapproval of their refusal to cooperate. In reply to WR's letter, the commission assured him it wished to work with the executive branch but did not desire to be harassed.[5]

This commission was more independent than others, because a constitutional amendment had been enacted to "remove it from politics." Rockefeller felt that the commission's "independence" made its members feel that they were independent of the taxpayers and everyone else.

The Game and Fish Commission invited WR to confer, but Rockefeller had a plan he liked better. He wrote to the commission asking all eight members to resign. One commissioner described Rockefeller's letter as "polite." Another said what they all felt: "I don't believe he can make us leave." And he couldn't, but he would only come to realize it after an agonizing time of hearings and pressures he initiated out of a belief that it could be done.[6]

Asked by the press whether he included the commission's executive director, Hugh Hackler, in his charges of misconduct, Rockefeller replied, "I think that Hackler is part of the total structure of the Game and Fish Commission. And once we get on a basis where we can take a look at the fulfillment of the Commission in its role as set forth by law, I think you will find that Mr. Hackler probably doesn't qualify for the job he is doing."[7]

The commissioners stood fast. No resignations were forthcoming. WR met this silent defiance by announcing that he would hold a hearing to investigate the commission. "I am pursuing this course for the people of Arkansas," he said, "and for no other reason."[8] But the commissioners, at least, didn't believe him.

The press loved the prospect of a colorful, controversial hearing, and they began pressuring Rockefeller about it. They recalled his earlier statement about repealing the amendment establishing the commission's independence, but the governor was beginning to be a bit more cautious. Though he retracted the statement he would hear of it again and again. Meanwhile, the commissioners were beginning to compete with the governor for space in the news columns. Two of them, using the old Democrat versus Republican issue, charged that the governor was trying to "fire" them because they wouldn't agree to give the Republicans "half of the Game and Fish jobs."[9]

Rockefeller countered that threat by asking the president of the Arkansas Judicial Council to recommend three persons to act as referees. Game and Fish Commissioner Raymond Farris, telling the press that the commissioners wanted to reason with Rockefeller, speculated that such a meeting would be of greater service than "this witch-burning."

But the governor persisted. He was determined to hold the hearing, and he hoped it could be held quickly. However, since no precedent existed for the hearing, legal ground rules had to be set and other matters attended to before the charges and defense could be heard. Rockefeller resigned himself to the inevitable delays, postponements, and general foot-dragging that seemed to attend everything different he tried to do in state government.

The press, as frustrated as was the governor about the delay, and thirsting for a new lead or two, began asking what the charges would be and who was going to be charged. But Rockefeller, more cautious now, stayed with his general charge of "misconduct," suggesting that though a couple of the commissioners might be singled out, all were "equally responsible."[10]

Meanwhile, Republican party executive director Altenbaumer, the one accused by the commissioners of demanding half the Game and Fish Commission jobs for GOP loyalists, was glad to continue the dialogue with the press while the governor waited for the legal wheels to grind. Altenbaumer challenged those accusing him of demanding the GOP jobs to take a polygraph test. He agreed to take one and said that unless the commissioners would too they would have to withdraw their accusations. Commissioner Hackler responded that he didn't need a polygraph to know that he told the truth.[11]

The Arkansas Judicial Council rejected the governor's proposal that it select a referee for the hearing, as did the executive committee of the bar association when the offer was made to it. Both groups thought the matter "tinged with politics." Determined to erase as much of the "tinge" as possible, Rockefeller set about to find the most impartial attorneys he could. On September 7, 1967, Rockefeller announced his hearing panel and evidence officer—the three panelists all being former presidents of Arkansas' bar association and the evidence officer a prominent trial lawyer.

The governor's rather lengthy statement was well received. One reporter wrote that the statement "sought to reinforce his [WR's] frequent insistence that the hearings would be conducted fairly and that partisan politics would not be a factor." The news report added that "the three referees are all Democrats and former Democratic officeholders."[12]

Rockefeller expected matters to proceed quickly from

this point, but the hearings were delayed when seven of the eight commissioners filed suit to stop the governor from proceeding with the hearing. (The eighth member, Lloyd McCollum of Stuttgart, was the only Rockefeller appointee.) The plaintiffs claimed that they were subject to removal from office only for the causes and in the manner set forth in Article 15 of the constitution, which is the general impeachment law providing that the house of representatives has sole authority to initiate impeachment proceedings and that the state senate must try impeachment cases. The chancery court ruled that Rockefeller's proposed hearings would be illegal and could not be held.

Naturally, WR appealed the ruling to the Arkansas Supreme Court, which upheld the governor's contentions, but refused to give him an immediate mandate to begin the ouster hearings. It was by now June of 1968, and more than a year had passed since WR began commenting publicly about the alleged abuses.

The next problem came from the findings of Rockefeller's evidence officer for the hearings. Many of the complaints against the Game and Fish Commission weren't holding up so well under close scrutiny. Three of the commissioners—Ed Gordon, Tom Pugh, and Lloyd McCollum—were apparently innocent. Evidence officer H. W. McMillan said that these three had been carefully investigated and that nothing could be found to sustain any of the allegations against them. "In fact," McMillan wrote in a report to the governor on July 15, 1968, "what we found refuted these accusations, and we feel these accusations are entirely without merit." Some of the others who had not been investigated quite so thoroughly by McMillan seemed about as innocent, and, of course, the file had been closed on one of the commissioners who had died.[13]

The whole episode, which began with wholesale reports of wrongdoing and subsequent blanket indictments, now seemed reduced to some charges that might hold up against a couple or three of the commissioners—in particular, Raymond Farris of Biscoe.[14] To say that Rockefeller was frustrated would be to understate the case considerably. He had been led out on a rather sturdy limb by eager aides—Republicans and supporters—only to have it sawed off by his own personally appointed evidence officer and the evidence, or lack of it.

WR now turned all his vexation directly on Commissioner Farris, who could be made a kind of example. He said the commissioner bought state equipment at reduced prices, used state employees for his private enterprise, and used the state airplane and state trucks for hunting trips.[15] The commission responded to this by releasing a letter from Farris' physician stating that the commissioner charged by Rockefeller was being treated for tuberculosis.[16] Sympathy for the man certainly blunted WR's attack as far as the citizenry was concerned.

There followed a lot of hassling about whether Farris was too sick to come to the hearings; but the governor, tired and disillusioned by the delays, nevertheless filed misconduct charges against two more of the commissioners, Chairman Ernest Hogue of Weiner and Newt Hailey of Rogers, and doggedly tried to move things along as fast as possible.

At the convening of the hearing, after a brief statement by the governor, three hours of testimony was presented on Farris' health. A physician said that he was too sick to attend; but Rockefeller's evidence officer brought forward five acquaintances of Farris who testified about having seen him at fish frys and other functions and that Farris had even "done a little fishing." Later, however, a physician agreed on by both sides confirmed that Farris was too sick to attend.

Another injunction was issued by Chancellor Kay Matthews (a Faubus appointee. Faubus had also appointed the commissioners Rockefeller was seeking to oust)—this one to stop the hearing because there were "rather strong questions" about Governor Rockefeller's power to delegate authority to the two lawyers who composed the hearing panel. The Arkansas Supreme Court would again overturn the chancellor and vindicate Rockefeller's position, but delay had been gained. In the interim Game and Fish Commission Director Hackler claimed that he had been offered a deal—that the hearings would be called off if the agency would hire the state Republican party chairman, Odell Pollard, as an attorney.[17]

That produced the desired effect—a shift of public attention from Farris and the other commissioners. Naturally, Pollard denied the charge and characteristically demanded the Republicans' favorite vindication, a polygraph test for himself and those charging him. Pollard showed up for the test, but no one else did; and the state police didn't want to administer the test anyway unless someone in authority—the governor, for example—requested it. With WR's directive, the state police did administer the test to Pollard, who insisted afterward that the test results proved his innocence.[18]

The Game and Fish controversy quieted down for a while, and it was not until late April, 1969, that the supreme court reversed Chancellor Matthews and thus cleared the way for Rockefeller to proceed with the removal hearings. Finally, the governor thought, he was about to get satisfaction. Two weeks later, however, Hackler resigned as director of the commission. A month later, Rockefeller dismissed the charge against Commissioner Hogue, because his term was expiring and because the charge against him was an isolated one.

That left only Farris and Hailey still charged with misconduct. When the new hearing got underway on July 15, 1969, the charges against Farris and Hailey were manifold: using a state-owned airplane and other equipment for personal pleasure, state-financed hunting trips to Canada, purchasing commission-owned vehicles before they were advertised for public sale, and similar abuses.[19]

When it was pointed out that Commissioner Hailey was in El Paso in the commission airplane, visiting a friend, two Arkansas friends testified that he traveled across the border to Juarez on business, to talk of hunting and fishing in Arkansas. When it was pointed out that he used the commission's plane to go pheasant-hunting in South Dakota, Hailey contended that he was trying to find out whether the habitat and climate in Arkansas were suitable for the breeding of pheasants. And to charges that Commissioners Farris, Hogue, and Hailey hunted elk in Colorado at state expense, the commission responded that the purpose of the trip was to see how Colorado managed its deer herd.[20]

The hearing also brought out the fact that Farris bought two used vehicles from the commission four days before they were to be advertised for public sale. Hackler said he had removed a Ford pickup truck and Jeep Wagoneer from the list of thirty-seven used vehicles to be advertised for sale because Farris brought him three signed bids on each vehicle. Hackler said he looked at the vehicles, thought he was getting all they were worth, and sold them. The two other bidders with Farris were the same on both vehicles. Hackler said he wasn't acquainted with them.[21]

Another charge was that a 7.2-acre cotton allotment belonging to the commission was transferred to a farm owned by Farris; Farris didn't pay for the allotment until the investigation of him began eight months later. A commission employee said a check from Farris to the commission arrived in the mail unsolicited, but he had no explanation for the delay.[22]

Commission attorneys, meanwhile, were contending that Rockefeller was personally funding the prosecution. They asked that WR be required to furnish a statement of who paid for the investigation, how much was being spent, and who had received the money. One of the attorneys also requested that the governor be called on to appear as a witness and to report on the financing of the hearing.[23] This request was denied by the hearing officers.

When the questioning began about Farris using commission men and equipment to do work on his farm, Hackler said he had learned about it accidentally while he and Farris were at a meeting in San Francisco. He said Farris had a telephone conversation in which he was told that "they" had taken pictures of a commission bulldozer on Farris' farm. "They" were field workers for the Republican party. An estimate of how much the work cost was quickly prepared, and Farris paid $1,229.31—some nine months after the work began.[24]

Finally, on November 4, 1969, Rockefeller announced that he had found Farris guilty of misconduct in office and had removed him from the commission. He wasn't ready at the moment, he said, to announce a decision in the case of Hailey.[25] The removal order would be appealed, but on January 21, some eleven weeks after the governor's ouster, Farris suffered a stroke. A short time later, he was dead. Rockefeller then dropped the case against Hailey.

Commenting in retrospect on the Game and Fish controversy, WR said:

> Because I was fighting the dishonesty and corruption of years, for me to take an arbitrary position would have undermined many of the things that I was attempting to do. So I went through this extraordinarily expensive and painful exercise to achieve the results needed, even though time and normal attrition were working in my favor.
>
> From the time I instituted these proceedings, the commission did more constructive things. They knew that they were being watched and that they could not get away with a lot of foolishness; and so during the period of my administration, we did see positive things and the elimination of negative things.
>
> The only thing that disappointed me in terms of the public was the fact that they could not understand the standards of

integrity or justice that I was attempting to demonstrate. They
didn't understand, as time wore on and no action was forthcoming, in spite of the fact that we were working night and day
with competent people. They didn't see results. Therefore,
they got impatient with me, not indignant with the law which
gave the commission immunity and insulation from the
people. They lost sight of this.[26]

Rockefeller's reform efforts in another area—hypocrisy
about liquor laws—suffered a setback right in the middle
of his efforts to get a mixed-drink law passed by the legislature. Trouble started when Senator Clarence Bell commented publicly that it appeared to him the governor had
had "possibly two or three shots too many" in his appearance before the legislature.[27]

The next day, in a press conference, the governor held
up one finger to signify that he had had one drink before
facing the hostile legislators. He said that his drinking had
become a political issue in the minds of some persons, but
that his drinking had not hurt his ability to serve as governor. In a press conference a day or two later, the governor
was asked whether he believed he made a political blunder
when he said that he had taken a drink before he addressed
the legislature. He answered that he had talked about
hypocrisy, and had he denied having had a drink he would
have been the biggest hypocrite of all.[28]

Rockefeller knew that his mixed-drink bill and the tax-
increase proposals would be received coolly by the legislators, but he was optimistic. Addressing the session,
Rockefeller said:

The most controversial item in the call is the proposal to au-
thorize, under certain strict conditions, the on-premises con-
sumption of alcoholic beverages. I am as aware as you are that
this is an election year but I am also convinced that the people
want this matter resolved and now. My principal reason for
putting this issue in the call is related to my respect for the law
and to my contempt for the hypocrisy which our existing law
has for so long encouraged and protected. I cannot serve as

governor in good conscience and not take a stand on this. Therefore, I am proposing a law that would abolish such hypocrisy.[29]

Rockefeller said his proposal to allow local-option elections on whether to legalize the sale of mixed drinks wasn't intended to change the habits of anybody in Arkansas. "To the contrary, my proposal strengthens local option. It eliminates the hypocrisy that has weakened our law enforcement." Rockefeller said his bill would "strictly regulate and tax heavily that which has been going on in Arkansas for years."

The governor was, of course, delighted when the mixed-drink bill passed. He had had some support from unexpected quarters in getting the legislation through the so-called "vested interests." They had been watching this Republican governor from the beginning. But they began to relax as the administration progressed and nobody was unfairly punished for supporting Rockefeller's opponents.

WR always believed that the economic power base needed to be mobilized and motivated politically to do the things necessary for progress. Thus, he didn't oppose the vested interests for having supported his opposition. Certainly he insisted that their requests be reasonable and right, but he also made it clear to them that everything wasn't going to collapse around their feet—that he was going to be selective. He would eliminate what was bad, keep what was good, and try to mobilize them to help him get his own measures through.

To a large measure his success rested on his ability to secure the support of those people. Rockefeller said:

In the days gone by, there were abuses of governmental management, corruption, and what have you. It was a never-ending thing. During the first term, we were in an adversary position. That was inevitable because some of the reforms we were undertaking had a very strong influence on the conduct of their business. In the second term, the relationships were much more relaxed . . . . So many of those people, who initially were afraid of the unknown, found that the unknown developed into a very definitely known and dependable quantity. And although they may not have gotten out and worked for my reelection, I am perfectly satisfied that many of them did nothing to aid in my defeat.[30]

But the same couldn't be said of WR's own appointees and their hazardous methods of operating. One series of events and their implications bordered on being a first-class scandal. It concerned the Alcoholic Beverage Control Commission (ABC).

Joe Gaspard, who had been a GOP field man for several years, was now the director of the ABC. A state police report dated October 15, 1970, stated that a man identified as Larry Case reported to the Little Rock Police Department that he had bought a quantity of hashish from a young (and newly hired) ABC agent who was related to a Rockefeller employee. The "buy" had been arranged by Earl Thomas, another ABC agent, who suspected the young man of being involved in drug trade. Gaspard had agreed to the set-up, according to the state police report, with the idea of determining whether the man was guilty—before the police did—and discharging him.[31]

According to the police report, Thomas called Gaspard after the purchase was made. Gaspard then telephoned Marion Burton, describing the incident to him and inviting Burton to his office to discuss which course of action should be taken. They confronted the young man and he wrote out his resignation, the report continued, with Gaspard then instructing Thomas to dispose of the hashish in some manner "other than burning it or throwing it in the trash."

After some further investigation, it appeared that Thomas might have been in partnership with the young ABC agent in a Little Rock night club and that two other employees of the ABC might have worked in the club while on the state payroll. The state police informed Rockefeller when they learned of the possible ABC connection with the club. The governor asked them to pursue the matter thoroughly and jointly with the Little Rock Police Department. The young ABC agent later signed an affidavit to the effect that Thomas was never in any way connected to the club, the state police report stated.

Marion Burton takes strong issue with the report,[32] saying he never discussed the matter in detail with anyone other than the prosecuting attorney, that he did not in fact meet or know the young ABC agent until after he was released. According to Burton, his immediate response when Gaspard called him at home the night of the incident was that the prosecuting attorney should be contacted. Burton maintains that he never altered his position in that regard.

Rockefeller's public relations office issued a memorandum to all personnel as follows: "The governor asks that from now on you do not under any circumstances discuss the ABC matter or anything else except possibly the weather or the time of day with the press. It is critically important that you honor this without fail."

But long before the ABC intrigue surfaced, Rockefeller had dealt with controversies equally threatening to his administration. Early in his first term, a delegation of lawmakers called on the governor in his capitol office to get his views on a proposal to legalize gambling. The meeting was lengthy, and the room was smoke-filled. When the lawmakers left, they felt they had the governor's word that if a bill to legalize gambling got to his desk, he would allow it to become law.[33] Rockefeller didn't understand it that way. He vetoed the bill. The lawmakers, already precariously involved in the matter, responded bitterly. The governor obviously had the popular side of the issue, and the legislators felt betrayed by his stand. WR told a television audience in March, 1967, that he was "bitterly disap-

pointed that the House and Senate passed this proposal in
such apparent haste. . . . Anything you may have read, or
heard, that sought to imply my approval is utterly absurd."
Rockefeller said that the measure was of doubtful con-
stitutionality and he wanted to discuss it at some length.
He refused, he said, to accept the argument that there
were only two alternatives—flagrant, illegal gambling or
gambling dressed up in the respectability of state sanction.
Rockefeller maintained, in what some of the angry lawmakers thought was a "goody-goody" speech, that flagrant,
illegal gambling could be stamped out in Arkansas "and I
intend to see that it is." He reminded the voters that he had
campaigned against legalized gambling in 1964. But WR's
opposition to the legislature on this and other issues early
set the stage for the administrative-legislative battles that
would characterize his tenure in office.

CHAPTER X

Harmonizing
the Races

Before Rockefeller came to Arkansas, blacks were not only not encouraged to talk with white leaders as equals, they most often never had the opportunity to talk with these whites at all. Rockefeller, because of his particular family background and tradition, was able to say things to the blacks that nobody from Arkansas quite could have said.

When he first came to Arkansas, WR found that blacks were treated with a special kind of "tolerance" that was as unequal as it was seemingly gentle. He had no tolerance for that kind of inequity, and he encouraged blacks to develop their independent capacities, to set up mechanisms through which they could become more productive.

Rockefeller's image in race relations was of great concern to his political staff throughout his tenure in politics. In May of 1965 I wrote an elaborate recommendation to the governor regarding that image. I outlined a plan to stage a conference of sociologists, anthropologists, economists, and political analysts; then conferences with the executive committee of the Arkansas Republican party; then a meeting with other GOP leaders in the South "to discuss what policies and guidelines the Republican party in the South ought to have in terms of race relations."[1]

Schools were scheduled to conform to integration guidelines come September of that year or lose essential federal funds. Because WR's image was hardly that of a fist-shaking defender at the schoolhouse door, I and other staff members thought that something was needed to blunt the edge of this political hazard. His background, his liberal identification, his birthplace, and other factors, I thought, would leave his opinions and feelings about the race issue open to misinterpretation unless he proceeded very carefully.

Calling for a statewide telecast after all the preparatory study, solicitation of opinion, and development of a position for WR, I urged him to publicly discuss the inequality of education in Arkansas, as well as the social implications of any attempt to desegregate. He should avoid being associated with the extremist position on either side of the racial question—dealing fairly and sympathetically with the Negro struggling for equal rights and with the whites who so genuinely feared the effects of school desegregation.

Neither the involved series of conferences nor the statewide telecast was undertaken. Rockefeller was clearly not as worried about his image in this area as was his staff. And even if he had been, WR rarely made decisions on the basis of the image they might convey.

When Rockefeller began making his first move toward the governorship, some polls were taken to determine what the racial climate in Arkansas really was.[2] In 1961 pollster Joe Belden discovered that 23 percent of the citizens called themselves liberals, 48 percent conservatives, and the remainder "something else or no answer." Belden said that the racial issue would be more important than usual with Rockefeller in a gubernatorial race. "The conservative label helps a candidate in Arkansas much more than it hurts him," Belden continued. "Segregation is confirmed as the most dangerous of issues for a politician in Arkansas. The public finds itself in an ambivalent position—and apparently expects a candidate for governor to do the impossible: do not mix the races, keep the schools open, but do not go so far as to disobey the law. Any candi-

date in Arkansas who openly espouses integration is asking for defeat, the results clearly indicate."[3]

People polled as to why Faubus won a fifth straight term
(in 1962) put "his stand on integration" at the top of the
list. In 1964, the people decided again that Faubus could
do the best job of keeping the racial peace. They liked his
style. Some agreed with Faubus' earlier public stand—that
integration ought to be resisted at any cost.

In September, before the 1964 campaign against Faubus
had begun in earnest, Rockefeller felt compelled to get his
racial views before the people. He sensed that they were
aghast or confused, thanks to the whisper campaign and
smut sheets that supposedly revealed his beliefs and actions on racial matters. In a statewide television and radio
campaign opening, he stated his case; he dealt with many
issues in the address, but race was a crucial one. Later WR
published the portion of his address dealing with race because the subject, he said, "sometimes is viewed with
emotion" and because "it is quite evident that my opponent is trying to inject emotion into the question by implying that he alone can give stability in these times." The
Republican candidate's position was stated this way:

> For three generations my family has been interested in the
> problem of race relations. Over that period of time my family
> has made contributions of many millions to segregated schools
> and colleges because of the belief that only through education
> can the races live in peace and harmony. Having been raised in
> this tradition, it is quite understandable that I should have
> been associated with an organization like the Urban League,
> dedicated to the achievement of peace and harmony between
> the races. My moderate beliefs are well known by the governor
> because I have discussed them with him on various occasions
> back in the days when we used to exchange ideas, and I have
> not departed from them, as he well knows.
>
> Any statements that he now makes to confuse you about my
> position are as unprincipled as many of the other desperate
> statements he is making in this campaign. I have been ques-

tioned on many occasions with reference to my policy on employment when I am governor. It is very simple. I will employ on the basis of merit.

In my appearance on the national TV program "Meet the Press," prior to the passage of the Civil Rights bill, I stated that I opposed it because of the police powers granted to the executive branch of the federal government which invade our state's right to solve our own problems at the grass roots level. When Senator Goldwater voted against the Civil Rights bill on constitutional grounds when it was adopted by the Senate, I commended him publicly for standing on his principles even though no doubt it cost him votes in various parts of the country.

When I am governor I will abide by the law because I must—I will have given my sacred oath to do so.[4]

Rockefeller was not a liberal, far from it. It may have been true—as some said—that he was color blind. The white liberal in Arkansas characteristically placed the black in a category just as unequal as did the segregationist. The liberal had his own kind of rules for relationships with blacks—never losing his temper, insisting at all costs that blacks be given the privileges they demanded regardless of merit, and otherwise accommodating all thoughts and actions about blacks to a preconceived structure. But Rockefeller operated in quite a different way. WR was and remained a racial moderate.

The governor's wife, commenting on her own and her husband's racial philosophy, aptly summarized their position when she said, "Our belief was that the average black person was intrinsically as able as the average white person, and the only difference in terms of performance was that the black person had not had the opportunities that the white person had had." She explained that Rockefeller did not want confrontation, did not want hate. "What he wanted to try to do was show these bigots there were outstanding black people who were competent. And he was also aware that most competent black young people had been leaving the state. They were leaving behind older black people who had not had much education or were not as smart or were terribly poor."[5]

He wanted to get the outstanding young blacks back to Arkansas, those who could become leaders. WR hoped that young, intelligent blacks would want the same things as young, intelligent whites—better things for their children. "No dream comes true until you make some starts," Mrs. Rockefeller said, "and so his obvious belief, proven through years of working with black people in other areas, led blacks to believe in him. They knew he meant what he said."

According to Mrs. Rockefeller, the blacks who worked with her husband were courageous forerunners of something the majority of the people did not yet believe in. These blacks were the objects of rude treatment coated with surface courtesy. Working under such conditions, she said, bespoke their maturity and their concern for their race.

"Because everybody was an amateur," she explained, "there were political bosses among the blacks, just as there were political bosses among the whites, and many people who worked for Win worked for the wrong black person, one who was supposed to be a leader but was not." There were, unfortunately though not surprisingly, many self-seeking blacks, she acknowledged. When her husband learned the painful lesson that he couldn't necessarily rely on just anybody's word, he began to seek personally those people he could believe in and trust.

Rockefeller himself said the black community had the feeling that he was a person who cared about them and was willing to fight for them. But still they looked for results, and in that sense he had yet to prove himself to blacks when he won the office of governor. They had had their fill of words, and Rockefeller would need to prove himself with actions. Even though he seemed to have the right background and the record for supporting their interests, they were still suspicious. Could he be believed?

They didn't know, but anybody was better than Jim Johnson. So the blacks, with a fair amount of organization into carpools, turned out in record numbers to vote for Rockefeller in 1966. The Republican governor-to-be had been quite careful in his statements, and blacks who supported him didn't do so on the basis of any recent pronouncements that they could claim as specific promises to them.

For all his liberal tags, WR had been more moderate in his beliefs than most thought. And many whites—as the 1966 election day neared—saw in Rockefeller a man who could keep peace between the races. But Arkansas' Republican governor was no more influenced by his white supporters than by his black ones. He had a philosophy about race relations that was not based on politics or expediency. He would reap some benefits from the expression of this philosophy in his administrative decision-making; but he would also suffer some losses. Some of the blacks exceeded his expectations and showed white Arkansas that a black could function effectively in a high position of responsibility. Some disappointed Rockefeller.

In his first term, Rockefeller asked the legislature to provide him with a council on human resources. The legislature refused, but Rockefeller wouldn't be stopped. With characteristic tenacity, he set about forming a council himself. He got it together and in September, 1967, said charitably that the bill had been defeated in the senate largely because of a misunderstanding of the basic intent of the legislation.[6]

Rockefeller denied charges that the council was merely a "disguised effort to promote civil rights interest in our state." He asserted that there would be no second-class citizens as long as he was governor. His honor was committed, he said, to upholding the civil rights of every citizen, and he wanted it clearly understood that he was "just as interested in the economic well-being of the Negro citizens of this state as of its white citizens; but not more so."[7]

The organization, for all its high purposes, never did much. Many believe that in this area of seeking to provide better opportunities for blacks and create better black-white relations, Rockefeller was at his best. But he functioned best in a more personal way, bringing his own persuasive powers and prestige to bear on particular problems. According to Bob Faulkner, WR's greatest contribution to racial harmony lay in his determination that the government take an active role in seeing that blacks became involved. He wanted more than the passive role of accommodating their demands. He initiated things. When an appointment would come up on a board or commission, he would say, "Let's have a black in that position." Faulkner went on to say that this active involvement of blacks in government "was basic to his [WR's] concept of right and wrong; it gets almost down to that. He knew—everyone knows—that blacks have been denied and deprived for long periods of time, and he didn't mind taking the guff."[8]

He got plenty of guff—both from whites who resented his color-blindness and from blacks who did. But he steadfastly held his firmly moderate position. One occasion that perhaps best typifies WR's behavior in times of racial crisis is the April, 1968, shooting of Martin Luther King, Jr. When word of the shooting reached Rockefeller, he cut short an engagement in Hot Springs to fly back to Little Rock for a rally on the steps of the capitol. He told the three thousand people standing in front of the capitol: "Let us not forget that we are all the creatures of God. Black, white, it makes no difference. Therefore, we must work in unity."[9]

About two-thirds of the crowd was black and a third white. State police and national guardsmen were stationed out of sight inside the capitol. After singing "We Shall Overcome" with the assembled people, the governor said:

> The problems that confront us today and the problems that confronted us yesterday, some of them will confront us tomor-

row. But maybe this tragic incident and the loss of this great moderate leader—a man who believed in peaceful leadership—will awaken the eyes and minds and hearts and souls of the people throughout our state and throughout the nation. I feel that Arkansas today stands at the threshold of leading the nation in a demonstration of what people of goodwill—God-fearing people gathered together—can do for a better America.[10]

The city police had come to Rockefeller earlier, to inform him that the blacks had asked for a marching permit. Rockefeller concluded that a march might invite trouble; at his wife's suggestion, he proposed the prayer service instead. Some of the police and Rockefeller's staff insisted that there was no need for him to get involved in the service. But Rockefeller insisted on participating, and Mrs. Rockefeller was beside him on the steps of the capitol.

Cecil Cone, the black minister who led the service, was fiery and volatile. Rockefeller said later: "When Cecil Cone begán to agitate after the meeting was over and just before the benediction, I just stepped forward and put my hand on his shoulder and in a very firm tone I said, 'I think now is the time for the benediction.' I don't think he realized at that time the very power that he had to lead and direct."[11]

Rockefeller was quite distressed by an article in *U.S. News and World Report*. On April 18, 1968, he wired the editor expressing his concern over the magazine's report "suggesting racial disturbances in Arkansas following the tragic assassination of Martin Luther King."

Regrettably, there was an incident in Pine Bluff. The other references . . . are misleading and unjustified. Arkansas, with the history of 1957, is justifiably proud of its conduct in this moment of emotion and tension. I believe that I was the only governor of the fifty states who held a memorial service for Martin Luther King on the capitol steps. In this spirit we are moving forward and hopefully will set a pattern for the nation, but such reporting as I have referred to in your publication makes our job unjustifiably more difficult and may even be a disservice to those of us who are sincere.[12]

Rockefeller tried in more than one way to keep racial violence in check, and for the most part he succeeded. One method, which some of the more hawkish and police-oriented on his staff talked him into, was keeping a list of campus militants. The idea seemed harmless enough, but Rockefeller would come to regret that he ever got a list together. And he would regret even more that he ever mentioned the list publicly.

In December, 1969, some reporters noticed Rockefeller aides interviewing young picketers in front of the Arlington Hotel in Hot Springs, where the Republican National Governors Conference was meeting. They asked Rockefeller about it. With his typical candor, Rockefeller said he liked the idea of creating national information centers to deal with traveling campus militants and that he was building up a file of information in order to be prepared for possible campus violence. For the first time in the state's history, the governor said, he had been able to coordinate college campus problems with his office. A series of meetings between WR and various college presidents had established a system of quick communications between the colleges and the governor. Rockefeller described it as preventive medicine, saying he didn't want to wait until problems developed to take any action. Rockefeller went on to say his office had identified a notorious campus agitator that a state college was about to hire. "After we identified him the college hired someone else."[13]

Ken McKee, a lawman and security investigator for Rockefeller, was in charge of the problem. McKee had been in the center of nearly every civil rights activity in Arkansas. He had one of the most detailed files available on militants and kept it dated for easy reference. Rockefeller soon saw, however, that he had opened a Pandora's Box

and found himself saying that his new system for compil-
ing information on campus militants was "informal."
Rockefeller insisted that the file being built up by McKee, a
former state trooper, was not a black list and that "there
was no suggestion of gestapo tactics" in it.

Press criticism mushroomed. The list was attacked from
other quarters as well. According to Hayes McClerkin of
Texarkana, the list Rockefeller was gathering "could be
used to intimidate persons." McClerkin, who would later
lose a race for the Democratic nomination to oppose
Rockefeller, said the governor's list of campus militants
was "not a healthy thing," especially if it was ever made
public. According to McClerkin the list could also be used
to discredit "those who may be guilty of no more than a
disagreement with the Governor."[14] The Arkansas Conference of the American Association of University Professors
condemned Rockefeller's list, saying that its existence
served to inhibit healthy dissent.[15]

Rockefeller got unwanted praise from the hard-nosed
conservative elements in Arkansas—people who could be
expected to agree with the idea of keeping such lists of
trouble-makers.

As criticism of the list gained momentum, WR and his
staff began to assess ways of dealing with the problem. I
advised the governor not to back down from his position on
the list. As the chief executive, he was, I felt, bound to try
to prevent disorders and strife. Rather than suggest that to
compile the list was wrong, I advised him to "defend it as a
collection of names of real destructive types—lawbreakers
or those likely to be, according to standard law enforcement criteria for evaluating such probabilities. The big
furor from a comparatively small number of people has to
do with a general misunderstanding of who is on the list.
Burners and looters and persons who have demonstrated
by their actions that they might engage in such activities
are. If we can characterize the list that way, I think most of

the clamor—even from the liberal community—will sub-side."[16] But it never really did subside after that. There was growing disenchantment with WR among blacks and liberals, partly because he didn't play favorites much, not even among blacks.

By the time of the "list" incident, Rockefeller's patience had worn a bit thinner than when he was dealing with the "Forrest City" incident some six months earlier. Then, Rockefeller would wait for three hours on one occasion to meet with a black minister from Forrest City.

It was July 30, 1969, and a racial crisis had been smol-dering in Forrest City for months. It threatened to explode at any time. And if it did, the governor's good image in race relations, his efforts to get blacks into better and more re-sponsible jobs, and the confidence in him held by the people of Arkansas would suffer a real setback. For these and perhaps other reasons the governor, who almost al-ways kept other people waiting, held his peace and figura-tively paced the floor in the mansion until it was obvious that the Reverend Cato Brooks wasn't going to appear for their scheduled conference. The next step, Rockefeller ad-vised newsmen, some of whom had also waited, was up to Brooks.

This crisis had formally begun in January, 1969, when Forrest City officials were presented with a list of com-plaints about segregation and discrimination by the Rev-erend J. F. Cooley, who joined forces soon afterward with Brooks. Cooley had a club of black boys in Forrest City that he wanted to help, and he taught social studies in the all-black Lincoln High School. Brooks, a minister, was unem-ployed. Within two months, they had attracted consider-able attention and were under verbal attack from whites led by Norman Saliba, a surgeon who was a member of the John Birch Society and of the school board.[17]

Saliba said that Cooley was using his classroom to en-courage civil rights activities and recommended that

Cooley be fired. He was. The next day about two hundred black students, protesting what they considered unjust treatment of Cooley, caused thousands of dollars worth of damage. Some of them were sentenced to state penal institutions; but those who were not prosecuted and some new supporters continued their protest.[18] In June they picketed the St. Francis County courthouse and initiated a boycott of certain white merchants in Forrest City whom they considered unfair to blacks.

The situation became more serious when Brooks invited a black militant from Memphis, Lance "Sweet Willie Wine" Watson, to join them. Rockefeller kept referring to him as "Wee Willie Wine," which didn't endear the governor to this angular and angry member of the "Invaders" who would attempt to organize a march on the state capitol.

The picketing and boycotting got results; within a few weeks Brooks claimed they had almost completely shut off all Negro traffic to the stores they were picketing. The city's chamber of commerce formed a biracial committee and urged the blacks to negotiate with it. Brooks and his followers refused. The county sheriff deputized seventy men, after which Brooks and "Sweet Willie" tried unsuccessfully to get federal intervention.

They went to see the governor then. He was in Washington. An aide phoned him, though; and the governor said he would meet with the blacks. But he disapproved of their proposal to bring their problems to the capitol by means of a mule-drawn caravan and "poor people's march" to the statehouse, complete with songs, press, and trouble. "This is not a public camping ground," the governor insisted stubbornly, and he meant it.[19] When asked how he would prevent them from camping, the governor replied quickly: "With State Police." He said that he had been in touch with both sides and that he didn't think the problems were insoluble. He was reasonably confident that neither the march nor the capitol-lawn camping would ever take place.

Meanwhile, the Forrest City Chamber of Commerce, acting on the recommendation of the city's new biracial committee, voted unanimously to give increased consideration to hiring blacks. That wasn't enough. The tension grew. Rockefeller offered to act as "moderator" in the crisis. But he added that he wouldn't go to Forrest City unless leaders of both black and white communities felt his services would be useful. The Forrest City folks could never completely agree on that.

Rockefeller told the press that he had made himself available to meet with any groups that represented the people of Forrest City. When asked if "Sweet Willie" Watson fell into that category, the governor questioned whether Watson, being there as a visitor, necessarily represented the people of Forrest City.[20]

Brooks and his black followers said they weren't interested in meeting with Rockefeller unless he was willing to "do something constructive in Forrest City." Brooks maintained that Rockefeller had "sat quietly by and let the situation in Forrest City exist." Brooks and his people also expressed anger over the fact that the governor had talked to the mayor and the sheriff, "two of the biggest racists in the city," about racial problems.

Brooks announced shortly afterward that the march from Forrest City to Little Rock would take place; the 130-mile journey was scheduled to begin on August 20. There would be a rally at the state capitol on August 24, the black minister promised. The governor would be invited to the rally, Brooks continued; if he didn't accept, it would be taken as an insult to the poor people of Arkansas.[21]

Meanwhile, Rockefeller's tenacity had paid off. He announced that his offer to moderate the dispute had been accepted. He named a committee of fact-finders to visit

Forrest City and advise him about the situation there. Their report would serve as the basis for his decision about whether to go to Forrest City personally. He hadn't talked to Brooks, however, Rockefeller added. And he questioned the black leader's motives, wondering if he wasn't more interested in trying to lead a national philosophical movement than in solving the problems of Forrest City.

Brooks did attend the first meeting of Rockefeller's fact-finding committee in Forrest City, though he had not made it to his scheduled meeting with WR. When asked why he thought Brooks had avoided meeting with him, the governor suggested that he was perhaps being advised by "outside influences."[22]

It began to appear that the proposed march, which Rockefeller called "cheap and dangerous theatrics," would indeed take place. The governor had begun to see the march as a means for using the marchers "for the personal aggrandizement of a handful of militant, would-be leaders."

Brooks had indicated to reporters and others that he was in touch with the Reverend Ralph Abernathy in Atlanta and the Southern Christian Leadership Conference (SCLC). Rockefeller made several calls to Atlanta and confirmed his suspicions that Brooks hadn't talked with Abernathy. The governor also doubted that the SCLC had any interest in the march or the capitol rally.

Rockefeller's committee, meanwhile, wasn't being helped much by the governor's observation that Forrest City was experiencing difficulties not because it had tried to remain in the past, "but because it had failed to recognize the change of the present and plan for the future." After the first meeting of the committee in Forrest City, one black minister said he felt the discussion was "only putting out fires, rather than building bridges." Rockefeller said his own optimism shouldn't be misconstrued. He felt the meeting had not solved the problem. It only indicated to him that both groups had agreed to shoulder it.

Finally, Brooks and Rockefeller got together. After their meeting of August 11, Brooks called a press conference saying how impressed he was with the governor and that he had agreed to furnish the chief executive with a list of grievances, as well as solutions. Although Brooks said that Rockefeller hadn't asked him to call off the march, he seemed less interested in it after their meeting, and he agreed that it would be very expensive to have the national guard and state police along the highway to protect the marchers. "It would cost the state so much money, and we would rather them save their money because we are going to need it in other areas," Brooks said. He thought the marchers wouldn't be in much danger, because a lot of newsmen would be accompanying them. And, Brooks continued, "even though those people along the way are really segregationists, they don't want people to know how really mean they are, so they would be on their good behavior."[23]

Rockefeller and Brooks said they had talked over the issues of Forrest City—not the proposed march. However, after his meeting with Brooks, the governor withdrew his statement that the march would be "cheap and dangerous theatrics." He said Brooks had convinced him that "there is a constructive spirit behind the march." He went on to say, however, that he believed the march would not be held.[24]

Brooks insisted, if somewhat halfheartedly now, that the march would be held, unless the governor was able to "come up with something tangible" to alleviate the problems in Forrest City or unless the racial climate in Little Rock became "potentially dangerous."[25]

Another meeting between Brooks and WR was scheduled for a few days later. Before that session, the governor's public relations staff got to work on Brooks's list of grievances. The appropriate state official was consulted on each item, and a lengthy status report was prepared. The report contained either some proof that the matter couldn't be resolved or evidence that some action had been or would be taken. The document was given to Brooks at his August 18 meeting with the governor.[26] Brooks said the march was still on until he had studied the replies. He did study the report and then announced that the march was postponed for thirty days. Everyone breathed a sigh of relief—except "Sweet Willie" Watson. He wasn't impressed by Brooks's comment that racial tension was so high that the march might prove "unsafe and unpeaceful," or with Brooks's statement that the governor and his department heads had shown their good faith. Only a few hours after Brooks's comments, Watson announced that he would walk to Little Rock and anyone who wanted to could join him. As the march began, the town of Hazen reacted by closing down the community and arming 125 special guards to man streets that the city fathers had ordered blocked with farm machinery. When it became clear that only a few marchers would join Watson, however, the guns were put away and the machinery was moved back out into the countryside.[27]

As far as the militant blacks were concerned, Brooks and Cooley had sold out. Thus, when they announced plans for a committee that would need donations from across the state to carry on the fight for racial justice, very few donations were sent in. Rockefeller often seemed to be personally supporting a one-man aid program. And once that program began, it was almost impossible to stop—even after Rockefeller left office.

A group of whites from Forrest City, having lost patience with the militants, formed an organization called the Concerned Citizens Committee. The evening after Watson's march to Little Rock, about a thousand of them gathered outside the city hall in Forrest City. Several racial incidents had occurred just before the march, and emotions were strong. Three young blacks had been charged with assaulting a fifteen-year-old white girl; a white woman had accused a black youth of raping her; a white grocer had been robbed and stabbed, allegedly by five blacks. These events were foremost in the minds of the angry whites gathered before city hall when Watson and several of his supporters made the error of appearing on the scene. Watson was beaten severely, before he was rescued by Forrest City policemen; and Bonner McCollum, publisher of the Forrest City *Times Herald,* was also attacked. National guardsmen and state police were put on alert, and the atmosphere in Forrest City remained tense for several days. Shortly thereafter, Watson left Arkansas, and Brooks announced that his march was postponed indefinitely.[28]

After the 1968 election, the governor's image in racial affairs began to cloud. He seemed to falter in his efforts to please first the rednecks (they loved the "list" of militants), then the blacks. An *Arkansas Gazette* columnist wrote, "Governor Rockefeller appears to have cooled some of his Negro support by sponsoring the Riot Control and Segregation Lawsuit Refund Bills."[29] Although the second special session killed the bills, this columnist noted that many blacks were disturbed because Rockefeller put the items in the call at all.

"The introduction of the bills indicates that Governor Rockefeller is not really aware of the situation in the Negro community," one prominent black said. The blacks resented the state helping local school districts finance segregation lawsuits. They saw that bill as a means of delaying school desegregation. One black leader said, "The black community will take a closer look at him now. He had the Negro vote sewed up until he came up with these bills."[30]

That blacks had been appointed for the first time to responsible positions in state government and that Arkansas, which had not had one black member of a draft board when Rockefeller took office, now could boast the largest percentage of integrated draft boards in the country— these accomplishments of WR's administration were too

easily overlooked when his critics had an ax to grind. The
director of Selective Service, Willard A. Hawkins, received
a Legion of Merit award for the selective service system
achievement in Arkansas. William Walker was state director of the Office of Economic Opportunity (OEO). The first
black person to serve as the head of a state agency in Arkansas, Walker was also the only black state OEO director
in the South. But despite these actual evidences of change,
racial trouble remained an issue.

Rockefeller seemed "vague" to the blacks now. For one
thing, he appeared to be having trouble making up his
mind on busing. While it wasn't a dead issue in his mind,
in August, 1970, Rockefeller described it as "less and less
an emotional issue that leads to confrontation." He wanted
it to just go away, it seemed. And he believed it wasn't the
prerogative of the state "to move into situations" with busing problems unless the school districts requested the
state's aid.[31] Earlier he had endorsed the resolution on busing adopted by the Southern Governors Conference. The
resolution stated that the conference favored "quality and
nondiscriminatory education for every child" and urged
"restraint and good judgment in the use of any busing of
public school students from one neighborhood to another
to achieve racial integration." WR stated later, however,
that he had never "advocated busing to achieve integration."[32]

Tom Eisele believes that Rockefeller represented the
turning point in race relations in Arkansas. "I don't think
he was any different down here than he was in the North.
Nor do I think he came in here with the idea in mind that
'my purpose in life is to change race relations.' I think that
was part of his overall philosophy."[33] He was never pa-
tronizing to blacks; and when one didn't measure up in
some way, he received the same treatment from Rockefeller that anyone else would have. Ozell Sutton serves as an
example. A black man who worked closely with Rockefeller as director of the governor's Council on Human Re-

sources, Sutton—like all members of the governor's staff—had been instructed by the chief executive to stay out of politics. When Sutton used some office stationery to send letters supporting a black candidate for a minor Democratic office, his action was brought to WR's attention. The governor confronted Sutton with the letters and expressed his anger over the infringement of his staff rules.[34]

Rockefeller was equally angry over the seemingly unfair and arbitrary manner by which federal guidelines for desegregation were imposed on the school districts of Arkansas. He sent a telegram to President Nixon urging that HEW guidelines be applied to *all* school districts. Otherwise, the governor reasoned, school districts that had deliberately delayed and attempted to circumvent the federal guidelines would, in essence, be rewarded by the time extension and accompanying relaxation of requirements. Rockefeller expressed to Nixon his distress over reports that the administration planned to lift the deadline for ending segregation in the public schools. WR urged Nixon to reconsider, arguing that the action would break faith with the black community and compromise the position of those who had courageously gone ahead with objectivity and a sense of justice—if not always enthusiasm—in the implementation of federal desegregation guidelines.

He could be as firm with blacks as with whites, and was. Rockefeller didn't cater to either, though it sometimes may have seemed that he did, since neither race was accustomed to racial equality. On April 24, 1971, a silver plaque was presented to Rockefeller. An engraving of a photograph of the governor with a group of black youngsters appeared on the plaque; beneath the engraving was the following inscription:

> Governor Winthrop Rockefeller, an inspiration to the young, a symbol of security for the old, full of love, warmth and compassion; a champion of human rights, brotherhood and dignity, who brought the Rockefeller family tradition to Arkansas and

sacrificed time, resources, energy and public office for the causes of unity, justice and equality. Thank you for all you have done, for all you are doing to make our state the land of opportunity for all Arkansans. God bless you. The Black People of Arkansas.

CHAPTER XI

The
Third Term Bid

Toward the end of WR's second term it began to seem that he wanted his staff to insist on his running again. He was troubled by the idea of breaking his word and seemed to want whatever reinforcement he could get for doing it. Because his Statement of Beliefs had promised that he wouldn't seek a third term, WR was uncomfortable. He had not broken his word on anything of importance before, at least not to anybody's knowledge.

But as the time for making a decision neared, WR's associates became uneasy. Those who opposed the third term bid became more nervous, and those who were for it became more nervous, too—trying to rationalize their job-protecting interests by convincing themselves that the party needed WR for this third term. The GOP was in difficulty at the time and WR seemed the most likely healer.

If he won, there would be two more years during which the party would have a chance to build. If he lost, however, the party's problems would be worse than if he had chosen to retire gracefully. Facing the dilemma, some of WR's staff prepared a memorandum on October 31, 1969.[1] It sought to put the situation in perspective and was the culmination of many weeks of private agonizing and several hours of spirited debate, with not all of us agreeing on many of the points in the memo.

When the memo was presented to Rockefeller, he read over it slowly, for what seemed like hours. Finally, he closed the document, which was almost six pages long, and said, "There's a lot here." He put the memo aside, and a general discussion about politics followed. We talked about who the probable Democratic nominee would be (most thought Faubus); but we never really got into a debate about the big question, the third term. Clearly WR had decided to make his own decision.

Although the memo recognized some personal problems that might influence the outcome of the election—marital difficulties between the Rockefellers and WR's drinking, for example—the consensus was that he should seek reelection. The memo asserted that "the best interests of Arkansas and the Republican Party would be served if you do seek a third term." This was what Rockefeller wanted to hear.

Recognizing that Rockefeller's reform image had worn off and that there was less fervor among Rockefeller supporters, the memo asserted that the 1970 contest would not be easy. WR's aides believed that he should seek a third term but that he should enter the race with "at best a cautious optimism."

When Faubus and Rockefeller had locked horns in 1964, it had been a confrontation between the old and the new. Faubus was trying to continue the policies of the previous ten years—with the old guard, the inside guys, the cronies. Rockefeller was the indignant candidate against the machine, against a Democratic party that had become merely an instrument that operated to the advantage of Orval Faubus. But Faubus won.

In 1966, Rockefeller came back with determination, hoping and expecting that his opponent would again be Orval Faubus. He was ready for the six-term governor; he had files of data that could be used effectively. WR's own organization was ready to defeat this man who had come to represent the epitome of old guardism, of regressiveness, of self-serving government. But instead, Rockefeller faced Jim Johnson, a passionate segregationist, as articulate as Faubus but not the classic opponent Rockefeller was ready

for. WR changed his tactics and defeated the new opponent.

As governor Rockefeller set about to root out the old
guard and establish the kind of administration he had
dreamed and talked of. After the first term, WR faced
Marion Crank in his bid for a second term. Rockefeller was
running against the old guard again, and he loved it. He
was enthusiastic and disciplined. He inspired his organization with surprising performances—the campaign
opener at Winthrop, the television debate, his determination to win in spite of governmental footdragging and
legislative opposition. And he did win again.

In these four years he had made marks that the old guard
couldn't erase. His programs were good, and some were
tested, at least in part. The "Era of Excellence" was on its
way—late, halting at times, but on the way. Members of
the old guard had either dispersed or acknowledged that it
was possible to do well when treatment from the governor's office was only fair. But the much-vaunted machine
was broken, and people no longer expected handouts for
proper responses to the governor's programs. Rockefeller
had promised the voters that all he wanted was four years.

At the end of WR's second term, though, who should appear on the scene but Orval Faubus, the symbol of everything Rockefeller thought he had defeated? Suddenly, the
prospect of leaving his beginning efforts at reform in
the hands of their archenemy was alarming. And, in truth,
the prospect of beating the one man who had beaten him
could only be exciting. But more important than the idea of
defeating Faubus was Rockefeller's inability to let go of all
his efforts toward reform. He couldn't tolerate the thought
of Arkansas losing all the gains that had been made during
his tenure in office. Thus, he did something that went
against his grain almost as much as turning the state over
to Faubus would have. He broke his word.

In April of 1970 he wrote a letter to Republicans all over

the state, preparing them for what he was about to do: "I have not decided whether to seek a third term and I ask your continued patience," he wrote. "It is painful to admit an error and reverse oneself but my commitment to the Republican Party and to my own convictions is more important than my one statement. So if I decide that I can contribute more to our state and to our party by running for a third term, I am prepared to face the criticism sure to come as a result of the expression of that honest but nevertheless naive hope."[2] After WR's April, 1970, letter, I prepared a memo proposing a strategy for announcing the decision to seek a third term. I recommended setting up a political file of our most vulnerable areas and devising answers for each charge. The most difficult task of all would be explaining why WR was breaking his word and why the Statement of Beliefs was, in this detail, no longer accurate.[3]

There were other problems, too. A rift among the governor's staff had been developing for years. It expressed itself in an April meeting of one faction within the Rockefeller organization. This group, which was not "in" with Rockefeller, on an organized basis, nevertheless included some of his key people. They were concerned that his political advice was inadequate and incorrect; they believed that their views could benefit him. They agreed that the governor's political standing was at its lowest. Although they agreed that WR was the only Republican candidate with a chance to win, they felt that if his chances of winning a third term were remote he should step out undefeated.

The very fact that they met was an irritation to some members of the staff, and even though no words were exchanged, the tension heightened. Rockefeller was aware of it, and made an effort to keep things calm while he entertained the views of the "rump" advisory group in good faith.

On June 9, Rockefeller issued a formal statement, announcing his candidacy for a third term. He acknowledged that his decision represented a departure from his Statement of Beliefs. He said that all the rest of those beliefs remained unshaken, had even grown stronger throughout the period of sweeping change. He said he had spoken in good faith when he claimed that a governor should not seek more than two terms. But, he asserted, "if my commitment is to make our government the government of the people and keep us on the wonderful course of progress we are just beginning to enjoy, then my candidacy cannot be construed as breaking faith. I will humbly accept the judgment of the people. I am human just as are all of you. At times I long for the quiet days of work and the peaceful beauty of Winrock Farms but my part of this job is not yet finished. To quit now, I know in my own heart, would impose on me a feeling of guilt for the rest of my days."[4]

It seemed obvious that Faubus was in the Democratic driver's seat. WR's aides were confident of this, and the unused Faubus files were opened for the big campaign. Finally, it seemed, Rockefeller would get his chance. But disaster, in the form of Dale Bumpers, was to strike.

Blacks were gravitating away from Rockefeller, although in a May, 1970, poll, it looked like about 74 percent were still behind him. He needed more. In trial heats, Rockefeller's strength had waned also. Joe Purcell, the attorney general, got 48 percent to Rockefeller's 32 percent, and Faubus led WR by 44 to 42 percent.

In an August, 1970, memorandum, the pollster saw Rockefeller with a slight edge over Faubus, but the findings were inconclusive. The question plaguing the pollster and the Rockefeller organization alike was who would be the number-two man in the Democratic primary, since it appeared likely that a runoff election would follow. "Some candidate in the Democratic camp is going to rush forward in the next three weeks," pollster Newsom said. "It would seem unlikely that he could be Faubus or Purcell and is much more likely to be McClerkin [Hayes McClerkin of Texarkana] or Bumpers."[5]

After the primary, with Bumpers having "zoomed in," it became a simple question of whether Faubus could pull over the supporters of all the other candidates. Bumpers had offered little new, little that was appreciative of the Arkansas political situation; but he had an easy approach and a sense of relaxed freshness. Faubus appeared jaded.

Rockefeller's attack needed to be dramatic. The newness of Bumpers would have to be countered in some manner that would suggest an innovative approach to schools, welfare, the economy. The public had begun to demonstrate in an ominous way that it was impressed with Bumpers. In fact, Bumpers had an incredible lead of 70 to 20 percent, and there was a general feeling of Democratic ascendancy. The American Independent party's candidate—Walter Carruth—had made no headway, and the importance of the proposed constitution had not been impressed on the people.

Bumpers' appeal lay in his newness, and in the opportunity for a traditionally Democratic state to return to the fold. That, added to the fact that he had no record to run on, gave Bumpers a real advantage. It was apparent that WR must take the stage from Bumpers. The electorate was not nearly so much anti-Rockefeller as it was enchanted with the novelty of the Democratic candidate. A repeat of the 1966 and 1968 campaign techniques—with discussion of issues, standing on records, verbal disputations—was not going to win for the Republican side in 1970.

Bumpers was preferred 72 to 18 percent over WR for governor. There was no way to rationalize the gap between those two percentage figures. This would be a totally different kind of campaign from those of 1966 and 1968, because the opponent was different—unattached and unaffiliated. In a trial heat the count was 68 to 18 percent for

Bumpers. Clearly, the call was for dramatic, even desperate, action on the part of Rockefeller. Nothing was happening for WR in the public mind.

On October 26, the pollster told me that WR didn't have a chance. But on October 31, a fluke sampling provided a basis for this fantastic comment from Newsom: "The overall guess is that Rockefeller will be elected." The figures were 51 to 45 in Bumpers' favor, but the pollster saw the count as working toward a WR victory. "The race is closer than the opposition realizes," the pollster went on. "But the weight of probability still favors Bumpers. However, he has been losing and may very probably keep losing through Tuesday's election. A candidate who slides in popularity over the course of a campaign and whose intensity of partisanship is lower than his opponent's, in Arkansas at least, is not in the happiest of situations."[6]

Newsom clung to his early admonition from the day Bumpers won the runoff against Faubus; he urged WR to take a hard-hitting position on the issues. "Although it is very late in the day," he wrote, "I believe that a hard-hitting campaign on specifics for education—a very hard blow—might turn the trick and win the election on this issue alone."

But it was not to be. The Rockefeller organization knew that problems which Bumpers seemed to epitomize had had their beginnings long before the voters ever heard of him. Moves had begun months before to gently but determinedly push Rockefeller aside in certain areas, even as his power and influence seemed to wane in his own camp.

In July of 1970, the fight for leadership within the Republican party had already begun. It was going to be Charles Bernard of Earle versus Bill Kelly of Little Rock, and a violent but one-sided fight it would be. Rockefeller would support Kelly. He stated it publicly.

A "Draft Rockefeller" (for state chairman of the Republican party) movement began in Benton County. Bernard was quick to respond that he was still in the race and that he could not believe Rockefeller was serious about "stepping down" to the level of party politics after the heights he had reached as governor and national committeeman. There were rumors that the draft movement had begun in the Rockefeller public relations office, a charge WR vehemently denied. The truth is the governor did not want the state chairmanship, though several of his loyal supporters urged him to accept it.

Cass Hough of Rogers, one of the state's leading businessmen, a stalwart Republican, and a strong and consistent supporter of WR, was leading the effort to see that Rockefeller got the party's chairmanship. Hough, once he committed himself, was not the type to be easily dissuaded, even in the face of adversity. Thus, he was very disappointed and upset when WR pulled out of the race for the chairmanship with little warning.[7]

WR could have won—even the faction led by Bernard could see that—but it would have been difficult and WR just wasn't motivated for the fight that was shaping up. The man who had been defeated a couple of weeks earlier in his attempt to win reelection as governor notified Republicans all over the state that he would not accept the chairmanship of the party. He reaffirmed his support of Kelly, however. Bernard termed Rockefeller's withdrawal "healthy" for the party, and Rockefeller went before the Republican State Committee on November 21, 1970; in a misty-eyed farewell speech WR told the Republicans he had had "an emotionally rough time of it" since November 3. He said he didn't believe a single person had expected the results that came on that day and that no one had been harder hit by them than he. "But I have never been accused of being a quitter and I can assure you that I am not one now."[8]

The vote was 137 for Bernard, 28 for Kelly, and 27 for

Everett Ham, the former Rockefeller aide. Bernard went to the rostrum after his election, turned to Rockefeller who was sitting at his right, and said, "Governor Rockefeller, I say to you we do love you." He called the governor "Mr. Republican" and praised his accomplishments.

WR's aides felt like Bernard and the party had kicked Rockefeller's teeth in. Shortly after that time I sent the following memo to Rockefeller:

> Now that Charles Bernard has won the chairmanship, I expect him and all his supporters to begin professing all sorts of friendship to you and concern about your feelings with an eye toward maintaining your financial commitment or even increasing it to the party. You have been roundly accused by this group of using your money to create a "one-man party" and dominate the decision-making party processes. While nothing could be further from the truth, this argument had much to do with the Bernard victory. At any rate, I feel very strongly that you should NOT participate financially in the party under Charles Bernard to the extent that you have done in the past several years, and for several reasons:
>
> The party needs to revert to whatever it will be without your help. It needs to fall back to a new beginning so you can see what is truly there and can better judge where and to what extent you want to participate.
>
> You will be accused of "taking your money and going home" and other such things, but I feel strongly that this would be your best course of action. No doubt you will want to continue participating to some extent. If so, I recommend that you adopt a new policy—of matching the largest contribution by any other individual. That will certainly keep it from being a "one-man party" and will enable other Republicans to help share the financial burden.[9]

But the struggle for control of the party, which had begun before the election defeat, was only one of the internal problems Rockefeller encountered in 1970. In late September, before the third-term defeat, a former chief executive of the scandalous Arkansas Loan and Thrift Company alleged that Rockefeller and an aide, Glen Jermstad, had offered to pay for writing a book to incriminate former governor Orval Faubus in the AL&T scandal. Until that time, Rockefeller had been the beneficiary of all publicity about the company that went bankrupt and lost the life savings of thousands of persons. Rockefeller was now on the receiving end of some very bad publicity. According to Ernest A. Bartlett, Jr., Rockefeller and Jermstad had made a verbal contract with him for the book, and then broken the contract when Faubus failed to win the runoff.

Jermstad hotly denied the charge, as did Rockefeller, but Jermstad did say he and Bartlett had discussed the book. That discussion was incidental to a proposed financial transaction over land owned by Bartlett, but it didn't ring exactly true with the public. Jermstad, in anguished tones, declared that he was only a paid consultant to Rockefeller and that he had many business dealings that didn't involve the boss. He said it was a shame he couldn't get involved in other financial dealings without having his friendship with the governor brought into them.[10]

Rockefeller refused to be brought into the issue. He reminded reporters that it was his administration that blew the whistle on AL&T. He said he wouldn't be surprised if the Democrats were behind the whole thing, trying to embarrass him and Jermstad. And he added that Dale Bumpers was "a very nearly desperate man." Bartlett never filed the lawsuit he was threatening, but Rockefeller's troubles weren't over.

John Mitchell, then the attorney general, was quoted in *Women's Wear Daily* as saying that Rockefeller could defeat Bumpers because he could "buy enough votes from the far left or the hard right or the black vote."[11] Rockefeller couldn't believe Mitchell had said it, and the attorney general later denied saying it in a personal letter to WR. But the damage was done. Rockefeller had been embarrassed a few years earlier when it was revealed that checks from the Rockefeller organization had been written to blacks in Faulkner County and some other places as part of a carpool effort pointing to election day. Now here it was again, WR "buying" what he wanted and needed. Asked about Mitchell's statement, Rockefeller said he couldn't believe John could go home and face his wife after saying something like that about the people of Arkansas. The people of Arkansas are not for sale, Rockefeller added.

With that one barely settled, Rockefeller got another bit of "help" from Washington, this time of his own making for sure. Vice-President Spiro Agnew was invited to Arkansas by Rockefeller at the insistence of Jermstad and over the objections of other members of the governor's staff. Had he weighed the political impact of an Agnew visit? the governor was asked. Some speculated that it would hurt his position among black voters. Rockefeller chose to view it as "the support of the administration" but later conceded that the visit would alienate some Negro voters. He thought it would be fine if people would only stop and recognize that the vice-president was the second representative of the administration and was honoring the state by his presence and in support of Rockefeller's program.

Agnew was greeted by the governor and other dignitaries. In his speech he said that a "very attractive little lady" (a reference to Martha Mitchell) had asked him to "say it like it is about Bill Fulbright." Agnew then launched into a sarcastic tirade against Fulbright, to the consternation of the governor's staff, many of whom stayed in Little Rock. He commented on Fulbright's "radic-lib" friends and denounced Rockefeller's opponent as a "grin and grunt fella—the kind whose only claim to office is a simper and a skirting of the major issues." Agnew went on and on; he was interrupted thirty times by applause from the partisan crowd.[12] But elsewhere across the state, every word he uttered was hurting the Rockefeller campaign.

Election night that followed, in Rockefeller's office, was "a most pitiful sight," old friend Pickens said. "I was sitting there with him and members of the family, and we saw brother Nelson come on television holding up the V sign for victory. He was leading two to one, and Rockefeller was getting beat three to one. I saw those tears come out of his eyes like gumdrops. I couldn't take it. I just got up and went home. It's a shame to have a man rejected of his caliber, who brought this state to where we were all respected. They don't expect me to walk into New York barefooted anymore. They expect me to have on shoes."[13]

When Rockefeller came to the public relations office after his defeat it was a very solemn occasion. It was about 4 P.M. a couple of days after the defeat. Everyone was waiting for him in the front office. He entered the room, looked down the long hallway to where the office staff was seated, and stopped at a narrow table near the door. He picked up some fact sheets and other campaign documents and came into the office saying: "May I hand you a fact sheet; perhaps you haven't had a chance to read this." He was trying to smile. The women cried. The men looked away. WR said it looked like a wake was underway. "Somebody tell a funny story," he demanded. The office staff looked at Winston Beard, a research consultant, and somebody said, "Okay, Winston, tell us a funny story." He sat frozen.

Rockefeller sat down at the receptionist's desk and took a call from Governor Bob Docking. He told Docking as he ended the phone call, "I'm looking at thirty of the finest staff that any man was ever privileged to work with." His voice broke. He hung up and lifted a vodka and tonic in an attempt at a toast. Everybody started crying. To Rockefeller and all of those around him, this seemed a personal rejection, not a political defeat.

Faubus later analyzed the campaign this way, talking about the newness of Bumpers:

 All right, what's the advantage of anonymity? Every person who is discontented with a multitude of things—if you don't know that man's stand on that issue you think "he's my man. This one doesn't agree with me so this one perhaps does." And liberals can vote for that man, the rankest conservatives can vote for him, the middle-ground people can vote for him, everybody can vote for him.

Putting them all together, you know he can't fit the viewpoint of all these people—but because he keeps silent, doesn't take a stand, he becomes the beneficiary of all this discontent, all this desire to get rid of the things that are bothering them; and who else is there to take it out on, the man who is in, the man who is known, the man who is in power at the present time.

So I don't think Rockefeller had a chance in the world to overcome that kind of tide and then all these other things could be taken and magnified to contribute to that.[14]

Other factors contributed to the Rockefeller defeat. His forthrightness about taxes was influential. Although he didn't talk about raising taxes, his record of fighting for increased revenues was widely known and he didn't back away from tax talk.

Revolt at the prison, Rockefeller had handled with great skill and dispatch; but the obvious unrest there and the smell of trouble caused uneasiness in many voters, particularly in the areas around the prison.

The involvement of the congressional delegation also influenced the election. These men did not limit themselves to a television appearance with Rockefeller's opponent. They employed themselves and their staffs in an organized and systematic effort to elect Bumpers.

National trends had some impact on the election. There was a virtual sweep of Democrats into office, particularly in the South; and Rockefeller was in some measure affected by that. Bumpers was a Democrat the people could vote for. He offered a traditionally Democratic state an opportunity to vote the traditional party line.

Executive-legislative wrangling was a destructive element. Rockefeller's continuing debate with the legislature, in spite of all the progress made, was a cause of concern to the public. They had tired of controversy.

White backlash affected the election outcome. This was

a highly sensitive area. It seemed that many whites voted against Rockefeller for no other reason than that he enabled blacks to serve in positions of responsibility. This issue was connected to the very nature of reform government. From the day that Rockefeller took office, he served notice that old roots would be cut and old institutions fall. Any governor makes the normal number of people unhappy, but there was never a normal day in the course of Rockefeller's two terms. He confronted directly such issues as gambling, prisons, mixed drinks, blacks in government, and the pressing needs for new revenues. Each of these things took its toll among special groups.

And then there was the Rockefeller campaign style in 1970. In 1964 he had campaigned up and down the dusty roads, ducking in and out of every little fly-blown cafe and pool hall, sweating and tiring and obviously working his heart out. There was some of that in 1966, but he had backed up just a bit from so much personal effort. There was the bus to help out in 1966, and there was less street campaigning, more speeches in the shade on the courthouse lawn. He was going to the people less in 1966, asking them to come to him more. In 1968, his remoteness increased. He was on television to a much greater extent, trying to campaign through the media rather than in person.

In 1970 he pulled back to the limit. He campaigned through the media and in major rally speeches exclusively. Helicopters came into his thinking, with the hope that this could be a gimmick like the train in 1968. To campaign over the towns and cities of Arkansas from a helicopter through a loudspeaker system—without ever landing, just hovering, making speeches, and then flying on—this was his 1970 plan. Some of the staff tried to talk him out of it, and he did give up on the loudspeaker business; but the helicopter stayed in the plan.

Residents around the mansion were infuriated by the

noise of the big choppers—two of them—landing and taking off from the mansion lawn. A newspaper reporter wrote a feature about them, recounting the comments of one of those copiloting one of the machines—Jermstad—who kept talking about such things as "egress" and saying once for the Rockefeller admirers to get back out of the way because "we're going to physically take this thing off." It all went over badly.

Rockefeller's loss in 1970 was attributable to these and perhaps many other things, but an especially significant factor was that his very presence as a Republican had forced the revitalization of the Democratic party. He compelled the party to clean house and convert to a legitimate party. And when the Democrats did this, they nominated Dale Bumpers, who sounded the political death knell for Rockefeller. It is ironic that the very reforms he forced on the Democratic party served to defeat him, and doubly ironic that the reforms he instituted would be carried on in large measure by the man who defeated him.

CHAPTER XII

A Final
Act

Rockefeller agonized most of the day on December 31, 1970. He was making a very special trip, and he wanted to be ready—both emotionally and in terms of what he would say. He was going to death row at the state prison. He didn't have to go. There was nothing to gain politically. He had been defeated at the polls. And it wasn't likely that the men in that very special place were expecting him. After all, it was New Year's Eve and he had his own family. The prisoners knew he was different toward them. Over the years of his administration, they had come to see that Rockefeller was serious in his concern for them. But New Year's Eve?

Two days before, WR had commuted the sentences of all fifteen men sentenced to death. It was unheard of; this was the first time a governor had commuted the death sentences of all condemned men in any state. Now he was a politically defeated man on his way out, still trying to do what he believed was right. He was going to see them, but he was agonizing. "It was the most difficult trip I ever made," Rockefeller later recalled. "That's the hardest place to be on New Year's Eve, to wish people a Happy New Year behind bars. I had never thought about it. What do you say?"[1]

But Rockefeller said it right, as he most often could in such emotion-laden situations. He told them it seemed "extraordinarily inappropriate" to be wishing people in their circumstances Happy New Year. But he went on to say that he hoped the visit would maybe bring happiness. "I am here to let you know I am thinking about you and God bless."

Rockefeller had his son Win and Win's wife Debby with him, as well as a few friends and staff members. Sarver was there too. "It was a very poignant experience," the former prison commissioner said.[2] "Rockefeller was very moved. He walked up and down each barracks as well as death row. As he would walk up to the bars the men would come running from the back. Everybody crowded around the bars, reaching out to shake hands with him. He maintained his composure very well, but it was a difficult experience for him. All the men just wanted to touch him, shake hands with him and say 'Happy New Year.' We left there and someone suggested that there might not be time to go to Cummins and Rockefeller said, 'There sure as hell is time.' We drove to Cummins and he visited all eight barracks." Rockefeller said later, "Knowing that I was going out of office in less than two weeks, and knowing that many—particularly in the black community—felt that their hopes lay in my attitudes and philosophies, I didn't want to fade out of office and give them the feeling that I had forgotten them or that which I had stood for. So I think it was very important to my successor that my concern was genuine, personal, not simply a political concern."[3]

Rockefeller had known for some time that he would commute the death sentences of the men. "Before I was ready to take a definitive stand," he explained, "I did feel that it was important for me to have my position reinforced by the best that I could get of the professional evaluation of each individual case." Rockefeller said he had had to be careful; he didn't want to be branded a crusader and then be dogged to death.

WR had held his view of the death penalty for many years. On December 7, 1966, the governor-elect told a news conference that he was opposed to capital punishment because he didn't think it was a solution. "We ourselves admit to failure," he said, "when the only way we can cope with the problem is taking another man's life." A few days later, the Arkansas Prosecuting Attorneys As-

sociation unanimously adopted a resolution urging reten-
tion of the death penalty. Rockefeller said shortly afterward that even though he opposed capital punishment,
and would have broad powers of executive clemency, he
would not commute the sentences of the men on death
row. "Just because I disapprove of the law does not mean I
approve of ignoring the law."[4] But the statement rang hol-
low—to him and to those who knew him.

At the convening of the General Assembly in 1967,
forty-four of the hundred house members failed to take a
stand in a roll call vote on the abolition of the death penalty. Rockefeller asked the support of the Arkansas Bar Association in getting legislation to help in the fight, and
shortly after his request was made the house judiciary
committee did indeed vote "do pass" on a bill to abolish
capital punishment. But it was a year later, almost to the
day, before the electric chair was dismantled and moved
into storage and before the chamber where many men had
died was converted into a prison dispensary.

Clearly, the chair could be reassembled (one of the longtime prisoners knew how) on fairly short notice. John
Haley, Rockefeller's appointee to the prison board and by
this time the chairman, advised that the chair could be
quickly reactivated, though he didn't anticipate it. Haley
knew—like others close to Rockefeller—that nothing on
earth could make the governor direct the death of another
human being. Haley preferred the use that was being
made of the building then. An empty building serving no
useful purpose had been converted into a needed facility.
The prison executioner had been fired months before. Although no one except Rockefeller was absolutely certain
about what would occur, the electric chair, in use since
1913, had been retired permanently.

On April 9, 1968, Rockefeller said that executions of all
inmates on death row would be stayed until the United
States Supreme Court acted on the issue of capital pun-

ishment.[5] Seven months later, Rockefeller extended the
moratorium on executions until the high court settled
all constitutional attacks on the death penalty and until a
study of capital punishment in Arkansas was completed.

The house members grew tired of Rockefeller's "cod-
dling" of these death row inmates and on February 26,
1969, passed a resolution calling on Rockefeller and the
corrections commissioner to reinstate the electric chair or
resign from office. Later in the day they reconsidered and
voted to recall the resolution from the senate.[6] But it was a
fair statement of the views of many legislators.

In an earlier debate on the same subject, one representative had advanced an argument that may have been representative of the views many of the legislators held. He
said that he was a Baptist Christian and believed in capital
punishment, too. Electrocution would not destroy the
spirit or soul of men, he argued, only a little earthly taber-
nacle destined to death anyway.

Rockefeller, after his defeat in 1970, decided to complete
the business of insuring that his philosophy about capital
punishment became precedent in Arkansas to the extent
that he could establish it. Sarver said the question of
commutation had become more important as the campaign of 1970 progressed and Bumpers had declared himself in favor of capital punishment. Although he moder-
ated his statement later on, no one was really sure how
Bumpers stood. When the election was over, WR had
November, December, and part of January to make a decision. Morale on death row was very low.

In December, the decision was made to call in consul-
tants. Sarver was asked to attend a meeting at the mansion with Stanford professor Anthony Amsterdam and
others—including several lawyers who represented men
on death row, some of the governor's staff, and Haley. The
group met in the mansion sitting room, and the first to
speak was Amsterdam. He made an impassioned, articu-

late, beautifully phrased plea for the governor to commute the sentences. He spoke for some twenty minutes, after which silence fell over the room.[7]

WR answered that he had already made that decision. He would commute the sentences. But he wanted to form a committee to study each man's file and recommend further reductions in sentences. The choices were to commute to life, to commute to life without parole, to commute to something short of a life term, or to pardon.

This committee considered the files of the fifteen men under death sentences. The committee began early one morning and worked late into the night. They met again the following day. They ate their meals in the suite, so that the meeting would not be interrupted. Finally, on December 19, 1970, Rockefeller issued a carefully thought-out statement:[8]

> My position on capital punishment has been clear since long before I became governor. I am unalterably opposed to it and will remain so as long as I live. What earthly mortal has the omnipotence to say who among us shall live and who shall die? I do not. Moreover, in that the law grants me authority to set aside the death penalty, I cannot and will not turn my back on lifelong Christian teachings and beliefs, merely to let history run out its course on a fallible and failing theory of punitive justice.
>
> By the authority vested in me as the 37th elected Governor of Arkansas I am today commuting to life imprisonment the death sentences of the fifteen prisoners now on death row at Tucker Prison Farm.
>
> The records, individually and collectively, of the fifteen condemned prisoners bear no relevance to my decision. It is purely personal and philosophical. I yearn to see other chief executives throughout the nation follow suit, so that as a people we may hasten the elimination of barbarism as a tool of American justice.
>
> The records of the men on death row, along with the findings and recommendations of an outstanding committee I have empaneled, will now be presented to members of the State

Parole Board for their own consideration. I am aware that there will be reaction to my decision. However, failing to take this action while it is within my power, I could not live with myself.

CHAPTER XIII

The End of an Era

As the defeat at the polls soaked into his consciousness, there was a letdown. But WR was always moving forward, and in characteristic fashion he began to see things that needed doing in every direction of his private life. His infectious enthusiasm began to return, and for those he had left behind during his sojourn into politics, life returned to normal, with "Mr. R" once more on the scene.

As the fall of 1972 approached, a tired, rundown man was at the Republican national convention in Miami, looking back toward home, toward Winrock. An innocuous, marble-sized knot on the back undersurface of his right shoulder was annoying Rockefeller, and he had been instructed by his New York physician to have it removed. His New York physician had volunteered to do the job, but Rockefeller was chafing to get on to other things. He said he would have it taken care of as soon as he could by the family physician, Dr. Charles Wells, in Morrilton.

The knot had originally been discovered during a physical examination, and the New York doctor thought it was nothing more than an inflamed sebaceous cyst. Wells tended to agree. Otherwise, the examination enabled the New York physician to declare WR healthy. But Rockefeller hadn't been feeling well during the past few weeks, although he hadn't confided that to any except his closest associates. The otherwise good report on his physical in New York had given him every reason to feel good. Thus, he probably had no sense of foreboding as he arrived at the back door of Wells's office in Morrilton that late September afternoon. It was all going to be routine.

Wells used a local anesthetic and removed the knot right there in the office. "It was obviously not a cyst," Wells recalled thinking as he completed the minor excision.[1] But he didn't communicate his concern to Rockefeller. He walked WR to the back door and cheered him on his way. When the pathologist called Wells a couple of days later with the word that the "cyst" was a metastatic malignancy, Wells called Rockefeller and said he had a "matter of grave concern" to talk over with him. WR asked the doctor to "come right on up."

Wells canceled his appointments for the afternoon and drove toward Winrock, trying to think of the words he would use in telling Rockefeller. WR was waiting alone in the big living room when Wells arrived. The doctor cannot remember his words now, framed at the instant and spoken with not so much as a third person to turn his gaze upon for relief. "I tried to be frank, but not brutal," Wells said. The man listened without a word. Then he asked several soft questions. Wells said he couldn't answer any of them because there just wasn't enough information. They made plans to get Rockefeller immediately to New York for an exhaustive search for the source of the malignancy. Soon WR climbed aboard his jet, alone in the cabin with two pilots in the cockpit, and they flew away.

The laparotomy was done, and the incision was closed again. The worst was evident. His pancreas and liver were involved; his condition, inoperable. The only hope was chemotherapy, and that ordeal began. When WR was able, he headed home, with one stop in Little Rock.

So it was that on October 21, 1972, Rockefeller was standing before a fairly small group of friends and employees after his arrival at Central Flying Service. He had winged away from there many times on campaign trips, on business for the state or for himself. It was easy enough to remember all that if you closed your eyes, but if you opened them the visions of those days vanished. Here was a worn, tired, thin man, clad in a suit he hadn't worn for many years because he had long since outgrown it, standing on the steps of a strange airplane, the wind blowing the Hemingway-type beard.

WR put his hand on his son's shoulder then and told the group in a low, weak voice that it was good to be home. The son read his father's brief statement.[2] It told of the exploratory surgery, of how the findings had prompted the physicians to consider chemotherapy and radiation therapy. "I am delighted to say," the statement announced, "that seemingly the drug and I have hit it off like two wartime buddies and we have equal confidence in each other."

He was heading home to Winrock, and he regretted that his program would have to be one of "isolationism," the statement continued. But he countered the gloom somewhat with his characteristic optimism. The "isolationism," Rockefeller's statement explained, would continue only "until I regain my normal energy and vigor." If anyone were interested in his progress, a report could be obtained by calling Winrock. Meanwhile, he urged, everyone should go and vote. "I am going to." And he did, for the last time.

As the jet zoomed toward Winrock, several in the crowd began weeping. The crowd of fifty or so might have been much larger, of course. But just a small number were called. There was some resentment later among those not contacted, especially as it became clear that the appearance at the airport was their last chance to see WR alive.

Rockefeller was right about the therapy. For a while, it seemed to work wonders. Wells said it was possible to chart a definite shrinkage in the mass in WR's abdomen. Also, a nodule on his scalp disappeared during the treatment, and this was considered a good sign. The slightest improvements were noted carefully by Rockefeller, viewed by him and those around him with optimism; but the toxicity of the medication soon took its toll. His appetite disappeared and weakness increased. The medicine was discontinued. His condition deteriorated very quickly then.

He became increasingly sensitive about his emaciated appearance. Gene Young tried to get WR to walk about during the sunny hours of the days, to keep up his interest in the farm and the people, but Rockefeller would find some excuse not to go out until after the people were gone for the day. Young soon became aware that Rockefeller didn't want them to see him.

WR didn't talk fatalistically about himself, but Young said it was obvious to him that Rockefeller knew he would not recover, and he seemed most interested in determining where his remains would be placed, although he didn't spell it out in so many words. "He wanted me to do one thing," Young recalled, "and that was to get some property he had picked out in front of the museum, across the lake. He would joke about it. 'You think I want that for my remains, but I may use it for something else.'"[3]

WR's son recalled: "I guess Dad was a little bit Victorian about it. I don't think he really felt we should know exactly what he had, or exactly how serious it was. And if he wasn't about to say anything, I wasn't about to say anything."[4]

Could the son and the rest of the family have said, "Look we know you've got terminal cancer?" No. And so all of them, according to Winthrop Paul, played "a big game," with WR acting around the family—until very near the end—as if he had years to live.

Why did Rockefeller go to Palm Springs in those last weeks, leaving his beloved Winrock? Winthrop Paul believes the weather at Winrock was affecting his father badly. And maybe "he wanted to spare us the pain of him dying here." Then too, maybe WR really wasn't contemplating death as so many assumed.

Winthrop Paul says there was never one of those classic scenes, where the father sits down and says, "Well, son, I'm sick and I'm not going to make it." Rockefeller didn't really discuss it at all, and for that reason everyone else tried to keep up "the reasonably cheerful face." Winthrop Paul now says, "He may have thought the doctors were completely out of their heads, and that he really had five years. Who knows?" One aide near WR during the New York City Hospital stay said he was determined to keep the illness private. "He wasn't going to have all the little old ladies in Morrilton discussing his liver," she said.[5]

But Winthrop Paul had more to wrestle with than trying to keep a cheerful face. There was his mother, and he made a decision that created even more tension, perhaps hurt as well, in the final hours, the death and its aftermath. "I guess I took it upon myself that Mom didn't need to know," Winthrop Paul said, "because she had remembered Dad as a big, healthy, strong individual. She kept calling and saying, 'I'm coming out there.' Thank God, she takes trains, because she didn't get out there until after he had died. I don't know if Mom forgives me for it. But I still feel I did the right thing."[6]

All those in Palm Springs for the end found themselves restlessly moving about, obliged to stay in communication and therefore quite limited in what they could do. On the night before he died, they all went out to a pizza place to try to relax and have a pitcher or so of beer. When that didn't seem to be the ticket, they headed for a nice restaurant and a good meal; but nobody enjoyed that either. As Winthrop Paul remembers it, "We finally ended up with everybody in a vile mood. Nobody knew what to do." They went back to the Rockefeller home, watched television go off the air, went to their beds for fitful sleep. Early the next morning the hospital called. It was all over.[7]

It had been an ordeal of thirteen days since WR had gone to the hospital. Did he know it was his last journey? He confided nothing of what was in his mind as he prepared to leave his bed that last time. Maybe it was mere coincidence that when it was time to go, Ben Mitchell—longtime friend, devoted servant and chef who was far more than that to WR, who had struggled with every concoction he could think of for something "Mr. R" could eat—was there to drive WR to Desert Hospital in Mitchell's beat-up old station wagon.

When it was over, the family and aides got together their lists of people who needed to be called; each took some names and began telephoning, notifying friends of the death before they heard or read it elsewhere. Then they packed up and came home, bringing a cardboard box, six inches square, that contained the ashes of Winthrop Rockefeller, fourth son and fifth child of John D., Jr., and Abby Rockefeller. Winthrop Paul said that box of ashes was regarded "like a jar of nitroglycerin." He wondered, he said—and perhaps the others did—in a sort of rhetorical mental questioning: "How could you reduce such a man of that stature and size to this?"

They worked for four days on the invitation list for the March 4 memorial service, and they were grateful for the task, a thing to do that kept them functioning and pushing forward. They were ready for monstrous crowds, many more than the three thousand who made it up the mountain on that chilly, drizzly day.

They assembled quietly—all who could find seats—in the Museum of Automobiles, a mixture of the financial and political leadership of America, with those little old ladies from Morrilton and all sorts and sizes of folks in between. There was a short talk by WR's brother Nelson. Others representing various creeds spoke in orderly and restrained succession. But one—only one—was able to blurt out the thing that seemed trapped in so many of the faces there that day, held in check by their breeding or discipline or sense of place or whatever. William (Sonny) Walker, a black man, honored no such constraints. Argumentative, controversial, militant, forever demanding, WR's first important black appointment to a high position in state government—Walker was hardly the man one might have expected to bind together all the feelings present in that room on that day.

Yet, it was Walker who spoke with rough eloquence about the man who had put great confidence in him, during those earlier turbulent days as the struggle for racial justice in the institutions of government was just beginning. Walker's cry was a passionate one. "God be with you, Guv, until we meet again."[8]

Notes

CHAPTER I

1. Nelson A. Rockefeller, "A Tribute to Winthrop Rockefeller," March 4, 1973, in Winthrop Rockefeller Archives; and Little Rock *Arkansas Gazette,* February 23, 1973.
2. Little Rock *Arkansas Gazette,* February 23, 1973.
3. Winthrop Rockefeller, speech at an appreciation dinner on August 7, 1963, printed in a political broadside by the Reverend Corbett Mask in 1964; a copy of the speech is on file in the Archives; hereinafter cited as Mask, political broadside.
4. Little Rock *Arkansas Gazette,* May 10, 1968.
5. *Ibid.*
6. Resolution of the Arkansas General Assembly, 1957.
7. See the exchange of letters between Faubus and WR for March, 1960, on file in the Archives.
8. Little Rock *Arkansas Gazette,* February 26, 1963.
9. Little Rock *Arkansas Democrat,* February 19, 1963.
10. Little Rock *Arkansas Gazette,* February 29, 1963.
11. Associated Press dispatch, published in the Conway (Ark.) *Log Cabin Democrat,* February 20, 1963.
12. Little Rock *Arkansas Gazette,* February 23, 1963.
13. *Ibid.*
14. Little Rock *Arkansas Democrat,* February 26, 1963.
15. WR, speech to Young Republicans Club of Arkansas State College, February 28, 1963; a copy of the speech is in the Archives.
16. Jeannette Rockefeller, interview, October 14, 1971.
17. Marion Burton to Bill Spicer, September 19, 1963, in Archives.
18. Walter Stouffer, Jr., to "Fellow Republicans," October 13, 1963, in Archives.
19. Spicer to George Hinman, October 15, 1963, in Archives.
20. Spicer to Ab Herman, December 9, 1963, in Archives.
21. WR to Spicer, December 18, 1963, in Archives.
22. Spicer to John Paul Hammerschmidt and Gene Holman, January 13, 1964, in Archives.
23. Memo for files by Jane Bartlett, June 1, 1964, in Archives.
24. Everett Ham, interview, October, 1971.
25. *Wall Street Journal,* March 31, 1964.
26. WR, interview, March 26, 1972.
27. WR to Laurance Rockefeller, November 5, 1960, in Archives.
28. Jeannette Rockefeller, interview, October 14, 1971.

29. Harry Ashmore to John Ward, June 1, 1972, in Archives.
30. *Ibid.*
31. *Ibid*
32. *Ibid.*
33. A copy of this unsigned memorandum is on file in the Archives.
34. *Ibid.*
35. Ham, interview, October, 1971.
36. G. Thomas Eisele, interview, October, 1971.
37. WR, interview, March 26, 1972.

CHAPTER II

1. Ham, interview, October, 1971.
2. Sid McMath, interview, September, 1971.
3. Tom Eisele to WR, August 5, 1964.
4. WR, memo to files, August 11, 1964, in Archives.
5. Eugene Newsom, survey, October 10, 1960, in Archives.
6. Joe Belden, survey, February, 1961, in Archives.
7. *Ibid.*
8. Little Rock *Arkansas Gazette,* November 4, 1964.
9. Little Rock *Arkansas Outlook,* January, 1966.
10. *Ibid.,* March, 1966.
11. Little Rock *Arkansas Gazette,* October 15, 1964.
12. Transcript of WR's "Meet the Press" interview, May 3, 1964, in Archives.
13. Bethel Larey to Eisele, August, 1964, in Archives.
14. Boston *Morning Globe,* December 26, 1965.
15. Ward to Earl King, September 20, 1966.
16. Margaret Kolb, interview, October 21, 1971.
17. John R. Starr, interview, September, 1971.
18. Eisele, interview, October, 1971. Estimates of WR's spending range up to $350,000.
19. Ham, interview, October, 1971.
20. Little Rock *Arkansas Gazette,* November 6, 1966.
21. Little Rock *Arkansas Democrat,* July 21, 1964.
22. A copy of this flyer is on file in the Archives.
23. Little Rock *Arkansas Gazette,* October 15, 1964.
24. Mask, political broadside, 1964, on file in Archives.
25. WR, speech to Little Rock Ministerial Alliance, October, 1964; copy in Archives.
26. *Ibid.*
27. Orval Faubus, television address, October 22, 1964.
28. From interviews with Winrock employees, Rockefeller aides determined that a bulldozer operator under contract to clear portions of the farmland had accidentally run into the cemetery, which was overgrown from years of neglect.
29. There is a copy of this letter in the Archives.
30. Faubus, interview, July 6, 1971.
31. A copy of this pamphlet is on file in the Archives.
32. WR, interview, March 26, 1972.

33. WR to Faubus, November 4, 1964.
34. Faubus, interview, July 6, 1971.

CHAPTER III

1. Survey of public opinion in Arkansas, conducted in late 1965 by Joe Belden of Belden Associates, Dallas, Texas, copy in Archives.
2. WR, speech, June 14, 1966, in Archives.
3. Newsom, survey, May, 1966, in Archives.
4. *Ibid.*
5. Conway *Log Cabin Democrat*, September 16, 1966.
6. Newsom, survey, August, 1966, in Archives.
7. *Ibid.*
8. New Hot Springs study, 1966, copy in Archives.
9. Conway *Log Cabin Democrat,* September 19, 1966.
10. *Ibid.*
11. *Ibid.,* November 2, 1966.
12. WR, interview, March 26, 1972.
13. Conway *Log Cabin Democrat*, November 9, 1966.
14. *Ibid.,* November 10, 1966.

CHAPTER IV

1. Newsom, survey, January, 1967, in Archives.
2. WR, inaugural speech, January, 1967, in Archives.
3. WR, interview, March 26, 1972.
4. *Ibid.*
5. *Ibid.*
6. Faubus, interview, July 6, 1971.
7. WR, speech to joint session of the Arkansas legislature, February 13, 1967, in Archives.
8. WR, interview, March 26, 1972.
9. *Ibid.*
10. *Ibid.*
11. Searcy (Ark.) *Daily Citizen,* July 13, 1970.
12. WR, interview, March 26, 1972.
13. Robert W. Faulkner, interview, June 24, 1971.
14. Eisele, interview, October, 1971.
15. Jeannette Rockefeller, interview, October 14, 1971.
16. WR, interview, March 26, 1972.
17. *Ibid.*
18. Jack Pickens, interview, October 25, 1971.
19. WR, interview, March 26, 1972.
20. *Ibid.*

CHAPTER V

1. WR, speech to joint session of legislature, February 13, 1967, in Archives.
2. *Ibid.*

3. Little Rock *Arkansas Gazette,* December 6, 1967.
4. *Ibid.,* May 31, 1968.
5. *Ibid.,* October 28, 1967.
6. *Ibid.,* October 29, 1967.
7. WR, interview, March 26, 1972.
8. Little Rock *Arkansas Gazette,* May 26, 1968.
9. WR, to Arkansas Legislature, May 20, 1968, in Archives.
10. Pine Bluff *Commercial,* May 26, 1968.
11. *Ibid.*
12. Little Rock *Arkansas Democrat,* May 31, 1968.
13. Little Rock *Arkansas Gazette,* May 31, 1968.

CHAPTER VI

1. Bob Scott, interview, June 15, 1971, in Archives.
2. Rockefeller, address to the Arkansas Legislature, February 5, 1968, in Archives.
3. Little Rock *Arkansas Gazette,* January 17, 1967.
4. WR, speech in Sun Valley, Idaho, June 19, 1967, in Archives.
5. Little Rock *Arkansas Democrat,* October 27, 1967.
6. Scott, interview, June 15, 1971, in Archives.
7. Little Rock *Arkansas Gazette,* February 9, 1968.
8. WR, speech to department heads, April 5, 1968, in Archives.
9. Little Rock *Arkansas Gazette,* February 28, 1968.
10. Little Rock *Arkansas Democrat,* March 4, 1968.
11. Little Rock *Arkansas Gazette,* March 9, 1968.
12. *Ibid.*
13. *Ibid.,* March 5, 1969.
14. Eisele to Ward, February 3, 1970, in Archives.

CHAPTER VII

1. Margaret Kolb, interview, October 21, 1971, in Archives.
2. General knowledge circulated within WR's staff meetings.
3. Confidential source.
4. Little Rock *Arkansas Gazette,* September 25, 1968.
5. Little Rock *Arkansas Democrat,* September 25, 1968.
6. Harrel Hughes to Ward, September 26, 1968, in Archives.
7. Little Rock *Arkansas Gazette,* October 26, 1968.
8. Ward to WR, October 3, 1968, in Archives.
9. Little Rock *Arkansas Gazette,* October 8, 1968.
10. Marion Crank, television address, October 15, 1968, text in Archives.
11. Little Rock *Arkansas Gazette,* October 2, 1968.

CHAPTER VIII

1. WR, speech to legislative council, December 10, 1968, in Archives.
2. Little Rock *Arkansas Gazette,* November 29, 1968.
3. *Ibid.,* December 1, 1968.
4. *Ibid.,* December 11, 1968.

5. *Ibid.,* December 25, 1968.
6. *Ibid.,* January 26, 1969.
7. WR, speech to legislative council, December 10, 1968, text in Archives.
8. WR, inaugural speech to the Arkansas Legislature, January 14, 1969, in Archives.
9. WR, interview, March 26, 1972.
10. WR, speech to the joint session of the Arkansas Legislature, February 19, 1969, in Archives.
11. WR, speech to joint session of the Arkansas Legislature, March 10, 1969, in Archives.
12. WR, speech to the joint session of the Arkansas Legislature, March 2, 1970, in Archives.
13. Little Rock *Arkansas Gazette,* March 13, 1970.
14. *Ibid.,* March 12, 1970.
15. *Ibid.,* March 13, 1970.
16. Newsom, April 1970, survey, in Archives.

CHAPTER IX

1. Little Rock *Arkansas Gazette,* September 15, 1968.
2. *Ibid.,* September 24, 1969.
3. Conway *Log Cabin Democrat,* May 21, 1977.
4. Little Rock *Arkansas Gazette,* April 8, 1967.
5. Pine Bluff *Commercial,* April 13, 1967.
6. Little Rock *Arkansas Gazette,* May 30, 1967.
7. Little Rock *Arkansas Democrat,* June 1, 1967.
8. WR, statement, June 2, 1967, in Archives.
9. Little Rock *Arkansas Democrat,* June 4, 1967.
10. Little Rock *Arkansas Gazette,* June 7, 1967.
11. *Ibid.,* June 15, 1967.
12. *Ibid.,* September 8, 1967.
13. *Ibid.,* July 18, 1968.
14. *Ibid.*
15. *Ibid.*
16. *Ibid.,* September 19, 1968.
17. *Ibid.,* October 23, 1968.
18. *Ibid.,* November 3, 1968.
19. *Ibid.,* September 17 and 18, 1969.
20. *Ibid.,* September 17, 1969.
21. *Ibid.,* September 18, 1969.
22. *Ibid.*
23. *Ibid.,* July 25, 1969.
24. *Ibid.,* July 24, 1969.
25. *Ibid.,* November 5, 1969.
26. WR, interview, March 26, 1972.
27. Little Rock *Arkansas Gazette,* May 22, 1968.
28. *Ibid.,* May 23, 1968.
29. WR, address to Arkansas Legislature, May 20, 1968, in Archives.
30. WR, interview, March 26, 1972.

31. Captain W. A. Tudor, Arkansas State Police, to Colonel Ralph D. Scott, director, summary report of Case File C 25–165–70, October 15, 1970, copy in Archives.
32. Robert Shults to Ward, May 17, 1976, copy of letter in Archives.
33. Little Rock *Arkansas Gazette*, May 30, 1968.

CHAPTER X

1. Ward to WR, May 1965, in Archives.
2. Belden, survey, February, 1961, in Archives.
3. *Ibid.*
4. WR, "Statement on Race Relations," September, 1964, in Archives.
5. Jeannette Rockefeller, interview, October 14, 1971.
6. Little Rock *Arkansas Gazette*, September 25, 1967.
7. *Ibid.*
8. Faulkner, interview, June 24, 1971.
9. Little Rock *Arkansas Gazette,* April 8, 1968.
10. *Ibid.*
11. WR, interview, March 26, 1972.
12. WR to *U. S. News & World Report,* April 18, 1968, in Archives.
13. Little Rock *Arkansas Gazette,* December 27, 1969.
14. Little Rock *Arkansas Democrat,* January 3, 1970.
15. *Ibid.,* January 8, 1970.
16. Ward to WR, February 2, 1970, in Archives.
17. Little Rock *Arkansas Gazette,* April 20, 1969.
18. *Ibid.,* March 25, 1977.
19. *Ibid.,* July 4, 1969.
20. *Ibid.,* July 11, 1969.
21. Little Rock *Arkansas Democrat,* July 20, 1969.
22. *Ibid.,* August 7, 1969.
23. *Ibid.,* August 11, 1969.
24. Little Rock *Arkansas Gazette,* August 16, 1969.
25. Little Rock *Arkansas Democrat,* August 17, 1969.
26. *Ibid.,* August 19, 1969.
27. Little Rock *Arkansas Gazette,* August 23, 1969.
28. *Ibid.,* September 14, 1969.
29. *Ibid.,* June 2, 1968.
30. *Ibid.*
31. Little Rock *Arkansas Democrat,* August 20, 1970.
32. *Ibid.,* February 24, 1970.
33. Eisele, interview, October, 1971.
34. This incident occurred in my office, while I was serving as campaign director. It was not reported in the media.

CHAPTER XI

1. Ward to WR, October 31, 1969, in Archives.
2. WR to "Dear Fellow Republican," April 9, 1970, in Archives.
3. Ward to staff, March 16, 1970, in Archives.
4. WR, statement, June 9, 1970, in Archives.

5. Newsom, memorandum, August, 1970, in Archives.
6. Newsom, survey, October 31, 1970, in Archives.
7. Telephone call to me from Mr. Hough.
8. Little Rock *Arkansas Gazette*, November 22, 1970.
9. Ward to WR, November 24, 1970, in Archives.
10. Little Rock *Arkansas Gazette*, September 27, 1970.
11. *Ibid.*, September 19, 1970.
12. *Ibid.*, October 9, 1970.
13. Pickens, interview, October 25, 1971.
14. Faubus, interview, July 6, 1971.

CHAPTER XII

1. WR, interview, March 26, 1972.
2. Sarver, interview, 1971.
3. WR, interview, March 26, 1972.
4. Little Rock *Arkansas Democrat,* January 1, 1967.
5. Little Rock *Arkansas Gazette,* April 10, 1968.
6. *Ibid.*, February 27, 1969.
7. Sarver, interview, 1971.
8. WR, statement, December 19, 1970, in Archives.

CHAPTER XIII

1. Wells, interview, February 8, 1976.
2. Conway *Log Cabin Democrat,* October 24, 1972.
3. Young, interview, September 29, 1971.
4. Winthrop Paul Rockefeller, interview, February 28, July 12, 1975.
5. Ellen Ann Ragsdale, interview, February 20, 1975, in Archives.
6. Winthrop Paul Rockefeller, interview, February 28, July 12, 1975.
7. *Ibid.*
8. Walker, transcript of March 4, 1973, memorial service, in Archives.

Index